SMOKE SCREEN

PAUL PAPER

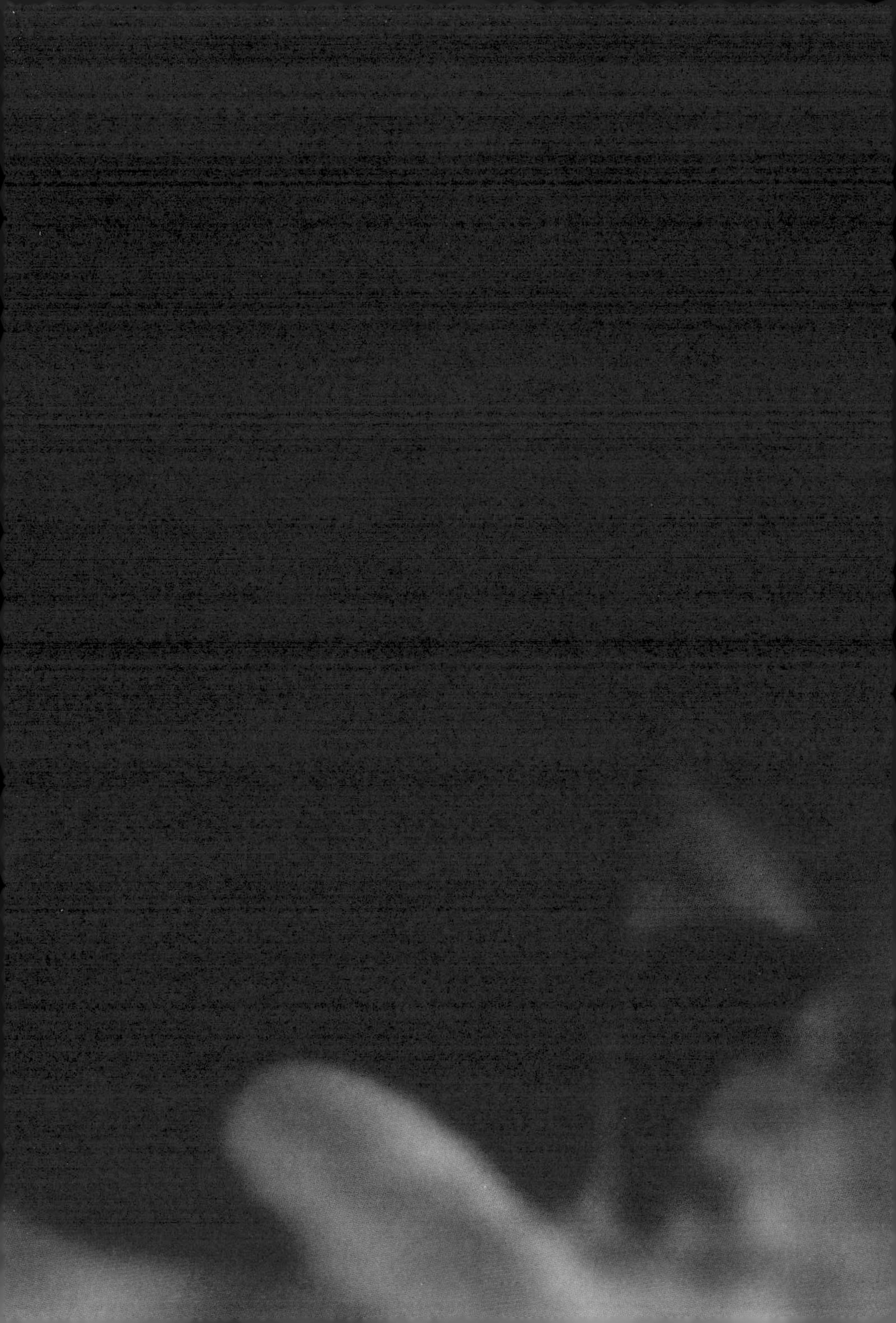

1

Smart Phone
Photographing
White Walls
Gallery Space
Tate Modern
Blank Image
Human Hand
Holding
Portable Information Device
iPhone 4s
Differential Focus
Left-Handed

Outdoors
iPad Mini
Tablet
Mini Tablet Computer
Portable Information Device
Reflection
Summer
Leisure
Idle
Skirt
Knees
Blank Screen
Screen

Close-Up
High-Five
Hands
Unity
Concepts
Corporate
Pixelation
Screen Capture
Agreement
Stock Image
Sky
Clouds
Stylization

John Berger
Hands
BBC
Art Critic
Art History
Photography Theory
Ways of Seeing
Blur
Out of Focus
1972
Screen Capture
Gesture
Warning

Message
MacBook Pro
Laptop
Computer
Notecard
Words on Screen
Hand Holding Note
Big
Fortune Teller
Zoltar Machine
Watching Film
Film Still
Success

Sunset
University Library
First Digitized Image
Laptop
Acer
Computer Monitor
Mouse
Desktop
Studying
Working Environment
Russell Kirsch
1957
Walden Kirsch
Open Book

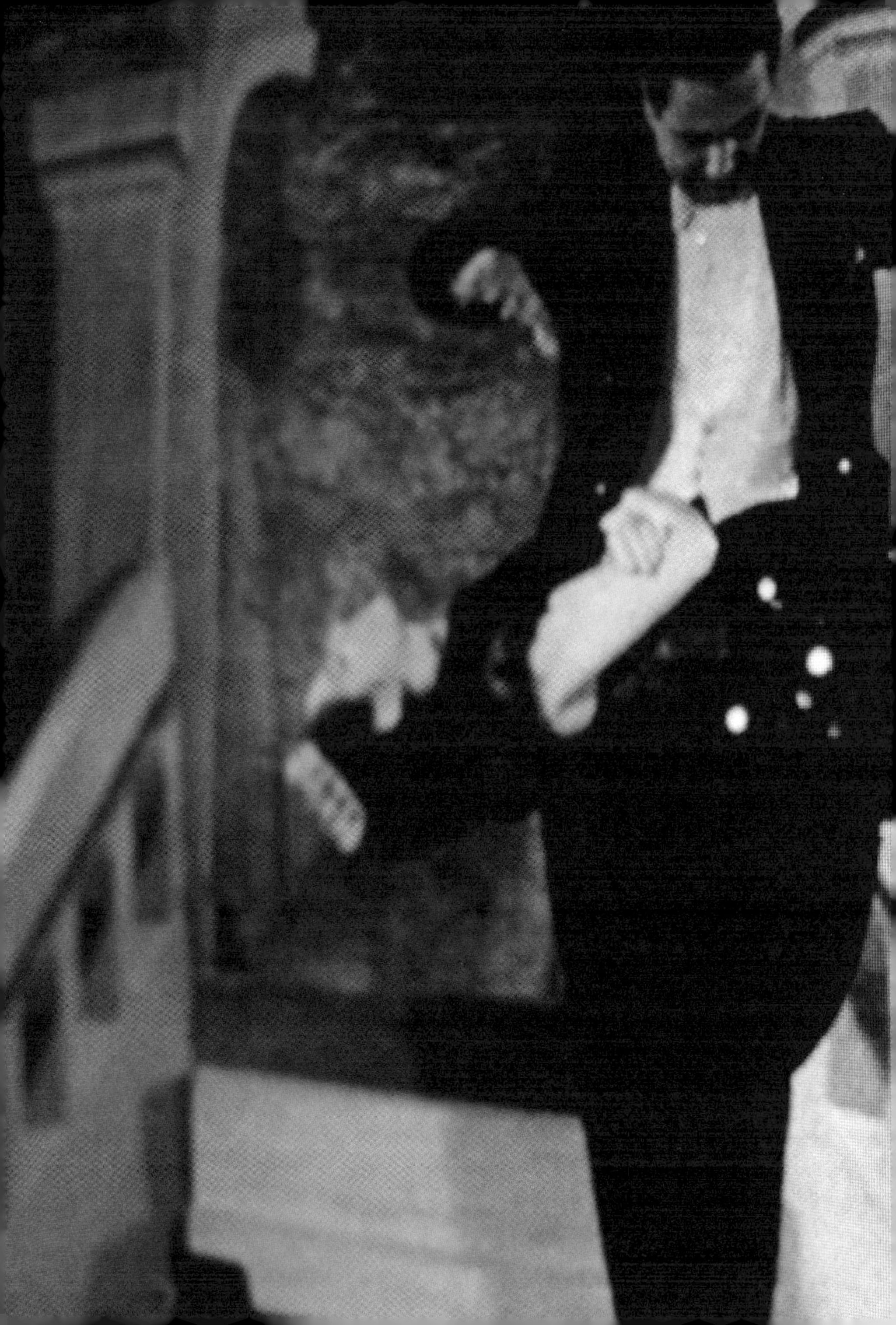

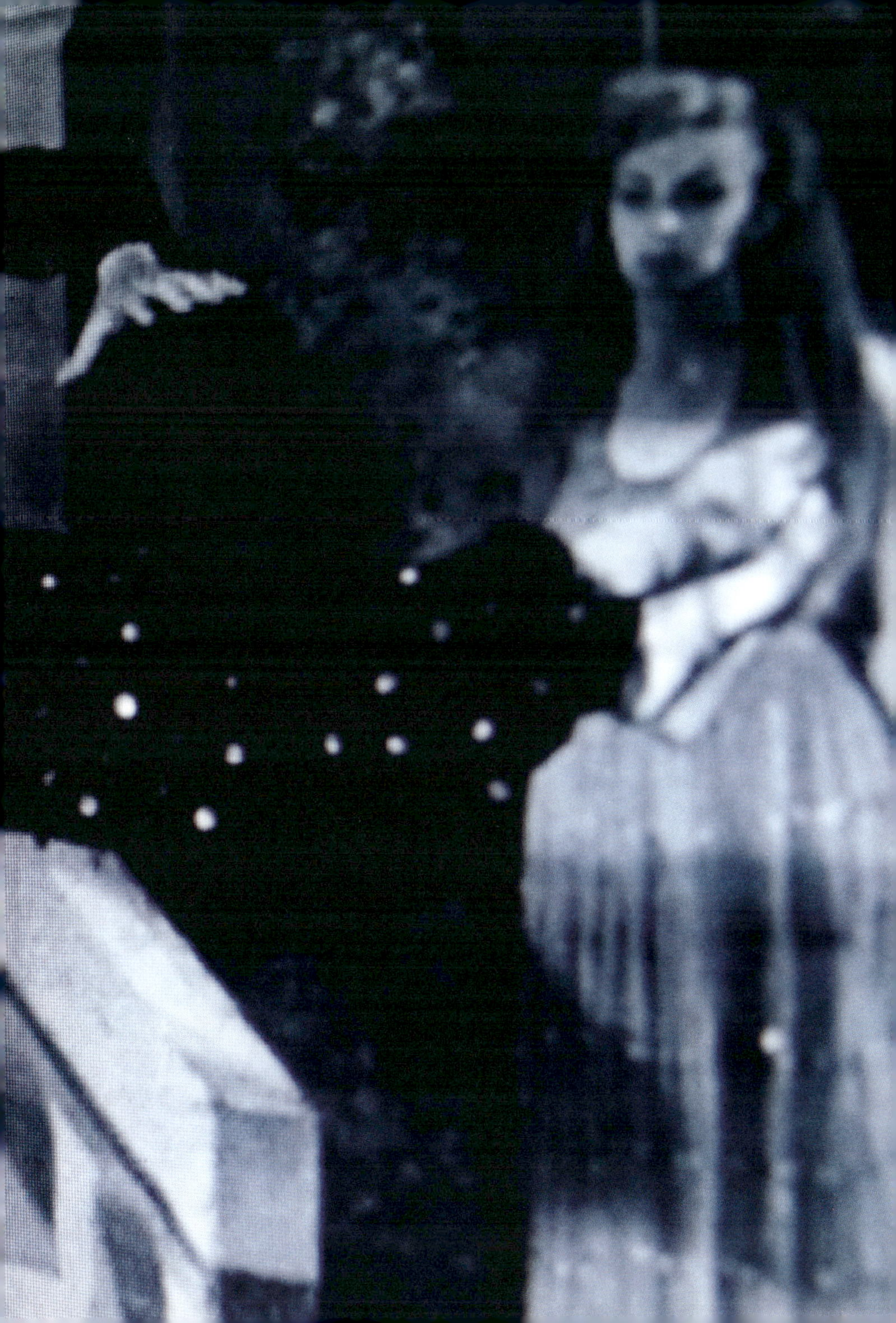

Participation

I am a screen chaser. I follow words across screens. I fix images on screens. I am a child of the screen and an adult of the screen world. I work and I make work on screen and for screen. I have headaches, strained eyes, shortened sight. I have back pain and neck twinges, I crane to see the screen. I watch screens, I touch screens, I never tire of screens.

I see delayed flight times and train platform alterations. Memes and games and clickbait. Shoes and books and leather satchels. Advertising and emails and endless petitions. Faces that haunt and figures that disappoint. Fierce words and lazy words, powerful words and weak words. Images that speak for themselves and images that stay silent.

I wonder if it is the screen that is watching me. The gaze of the screen hits the side of my face. It analyses me, reminds me, notifies me, compels me. I wonder if it is the screen that is touching me. The screen is cool to my fingers. It soothes my body heat, it appeases my anger. It placates me, gives distraction, offers me more space and time.

Touching
Touching Screen
Close-Up
Hands
Fingers
Boy
Persona
Film Still
Ingmar Bergman
Liv Ullmann
Moiré
Immersion
Human Face
<u>Participation</u>

Screenspace and screentime.

I am angry but distracted. I take photos, I write words, I read texts, I answer emails, I send messages. The screen presents infinite possibilities and limitless opportunities. I am hopeful and hopeless.

One day I disobey. I switch off. I shut down. I turn off. I exit.
I withdraw.

I refuse to participate. I start to participate.

Michael Jordan
Basketball
Shot Attempt
Black and White
Free Throw
Blind
Eyes-Closed
23
NBA
Chicago Bulls
Arm Band
November 23 1991
Solarization
Vision

Holding
Smart Phone
Google
Image Search
Screw
iPhone 4s
Human Hand
Close-Up
Portable Information Device
Left-Handed
Touching
Scrolling
Comparison

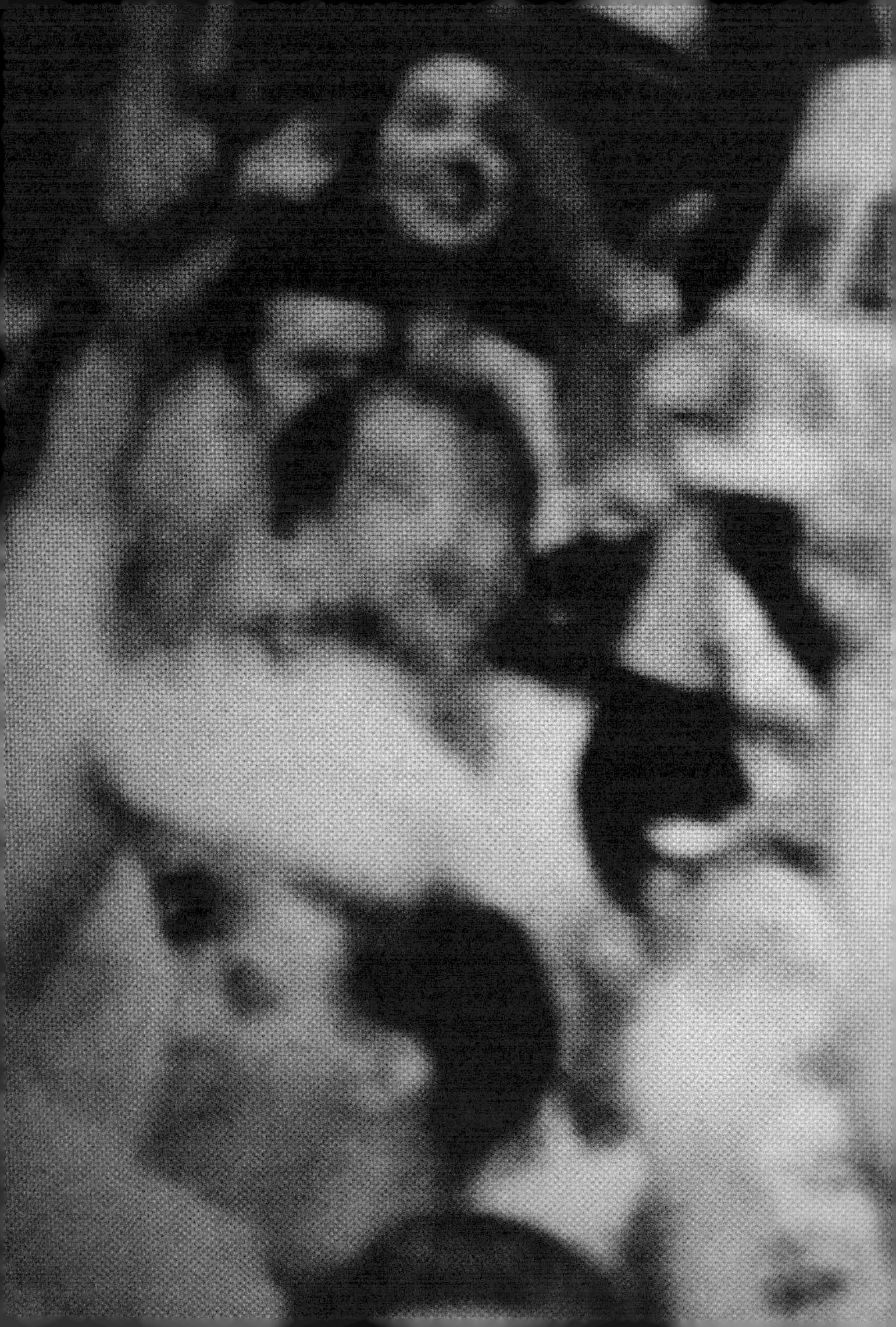

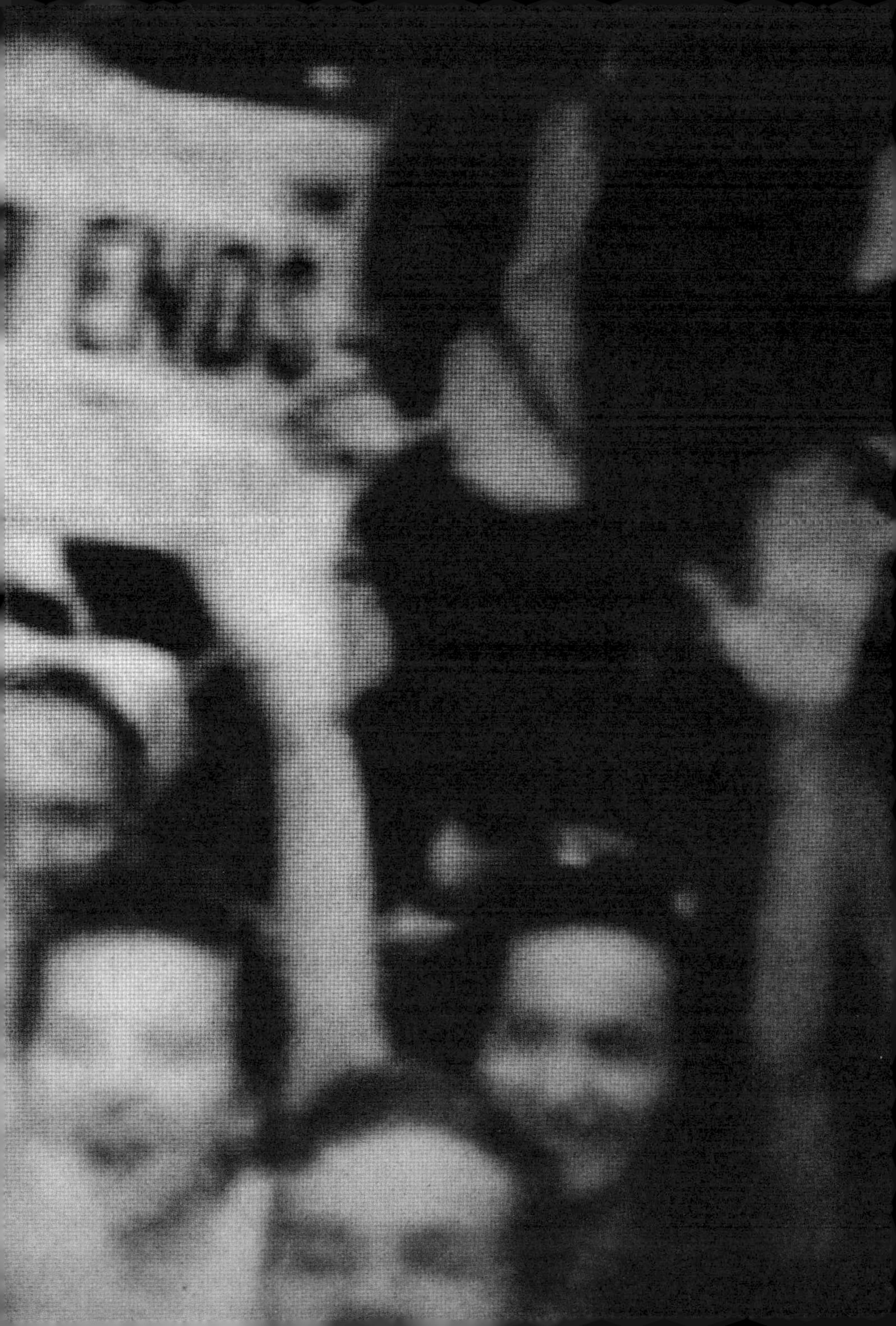

Tablet
Window
Text on Screen
Mini Tablet Computer
Translation
Dark Background
Rainy
Differential Focus
Holding
Indoors
Steamy
Blinds

Photo Messaging

VID-20150604-WA0000
Wow.
It is more blue than it looks.
IMG-20150604-WA0001
This one?
IMG-20150604-WA0002
Whoop!
IMG-20150604-WA0003
I thought so.
VID-20150604-WA0004
Haha so embarrassing.
IMG-20150605-WA0001
IMG-20150605-WA0002
IMG-20150605-WA0003
I didn't get any good ones. Soz.
IMG-20150605-WA0004
Ahhhhhh.
IMG-20150606-WA0000
IMG-20150606-WA0001
Just wanted you to know what I'm up to!
IMG-20150606-WA0002
We should have done before and after photos...
IMG-20150606-WA0003
IMG-20150606-WA0004
Oh man. Looks great.
VID-20150607-WA0000
Beuuuuuuutiful
IMG-20150607-WA0001
Another example

Jean-Luc Godard
French Filmmaker
Photographing
Photo Messaging
Moiré
Screen Capture
Black Hat
Lake
Glasses
Cigar
Holding Phone
Outdoors

IMG-20150607-WA0002
IMG-20150607-WA0003
What on earth did you do???
IMG-20150608-WA0000
On location again.
IMG-20150609-WA0000
It's finished!
IMG-20150609-WA0001
IMG-20150609-WA0002
I didn't want to look at it anymore.
IMG-20150609-WA0003
One more. With glowsticks.
IMG-20150610-WA0000

Smart Phone
Portable Information Device
Photographing
Hand Holding Phone
Image on Screen
Sunset
University Library
Window
Blinds
Photographing Nature
Close-Up
Interface

Screen Capture
0%
White Text on Black Screen
Pixelation
Close-Up
Data
Computer
Loading
Citizenfour
Film Still
Downloading Data
Classified Information
System
Textual Interface

Holding

I hold. It's smooth, carefully weighted and ergonomically designed to prevent fatigue, to keep me tapping for longer.

My palm is ballast. Fingers poise, dancers ready to ballet the invisible keys. Eyes slide - up, right, down, left, down. Unlocked.

It peals and I clasp it to my head, a bizarre appendage. It's a hot and inflexible block, radiating into my ear. Digits clenched.

Hands occupied. Lips stretched tight, jaw clenches, I bite. Too hard. Screen creaks. Something cracks against my teeth.

Instagram
Unfavoriting
Book Photo
Photo App
Smart Phone
Nokia
Lumia 920
Windows Phone
Touch Sensitive
Fred Ritchin
Interface
In Our Own Image
Thumb
Holding
Close-Up

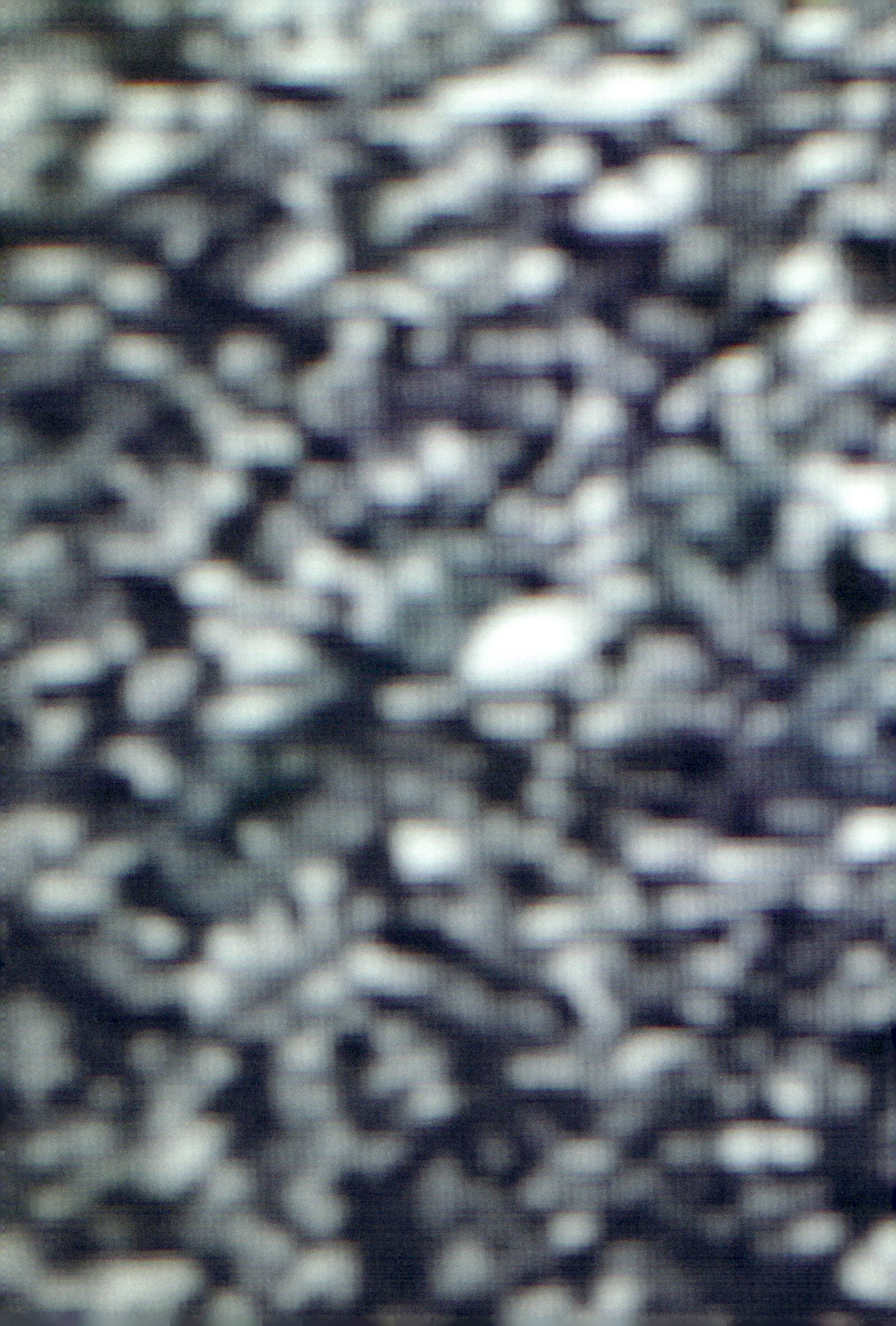

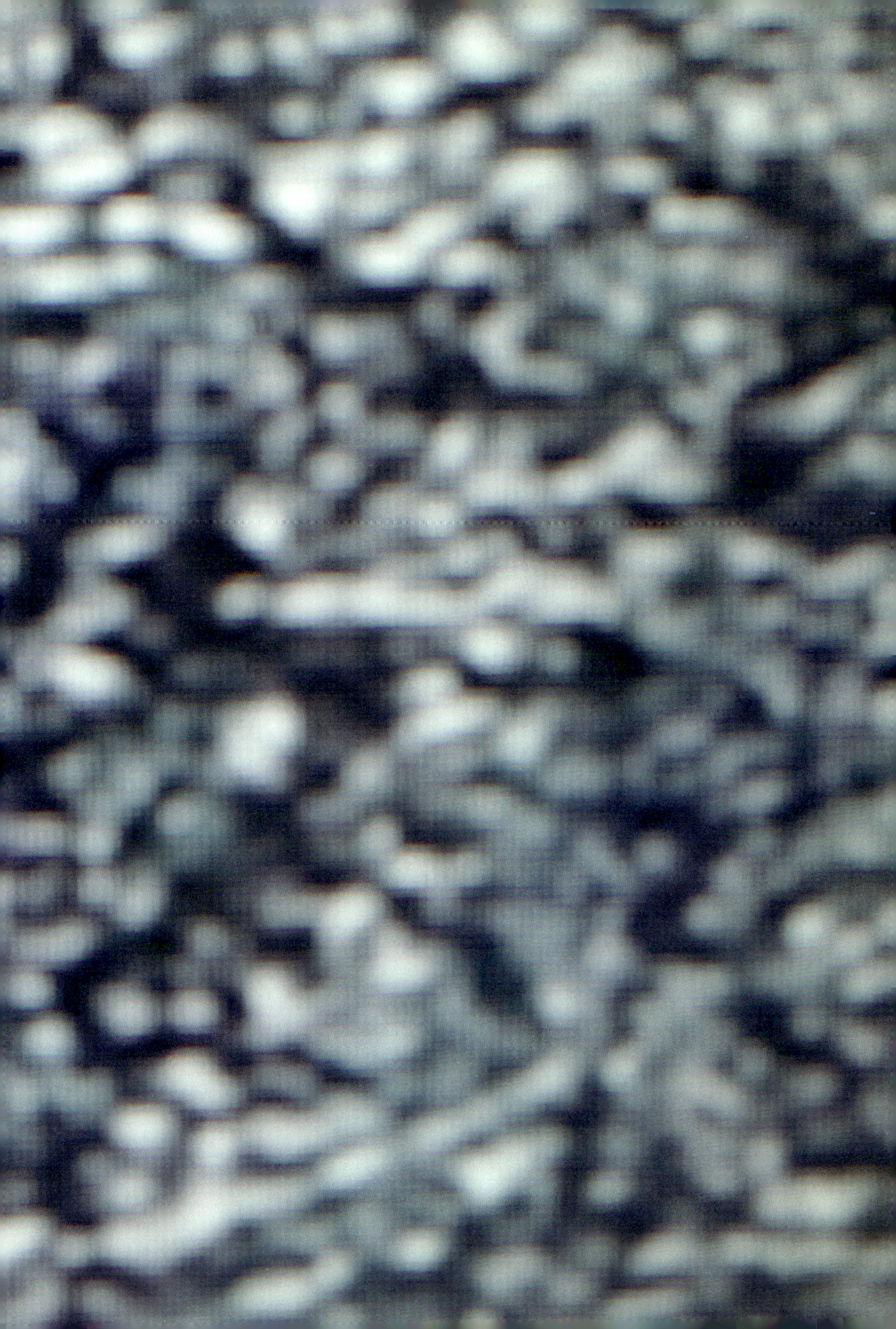

London
Bus
Window Seat
Selfie
iPhone 4s
Photographing
Canon
Analogue Camera
Gloves
Comparison
Photographing Self
35mm Film
Self Portrait

Film Still
Alfred Hitchcock
Rope
Suspicion
Gaze
Male Gaze
Plotting
Secret Plot
Screen Capture
Skewed Perspective
Human Face
Facial Expression
Farley Granger
John Dall

Portable Information Device

Name: indium
Symbol: In
Atomic number: 49
Atomic mass: 114.82 g.mol $^{-1}$
Electronegativity: 2
Density: 7.31 g.cm $^{-3}$ at 20°C
Melting point: 156 °C
Boiling point: 2000 °C
Vanderwaals radius: 0.162 nm
Ionic radius: 0.092 nm (+2)
Isotopes: 11
Electronic shell: [Kr] $4d^{10}$ $5s^2 5p^1$
Energy of first ionisation: 558.2 kJ.mol $^{-1}$
Energy of second ionisation: 1820.2 kJ.mol $^{-1}$
Energy of third ionisation: 2704 kJ.mol $^{-1}$
Standard potential: - 0.34 V (In^{3+}/ In)

Smart Phone
Portable Information Device
Painting
Photographing
Photographing Art
iPhone 4s
Pablo Picasso
Gallery
White Walls
Hand Holding Phone
Image on Screen
Tate Modern
Art History

Hand Icon
Click
Mouse Pointer
Screen Capture
Tornado
Jasper Tornado
Barn
Storm
Stormy Weather
Rural Area
Black and White
Photogenic
Extreme Weather Conditions
1927
Canada

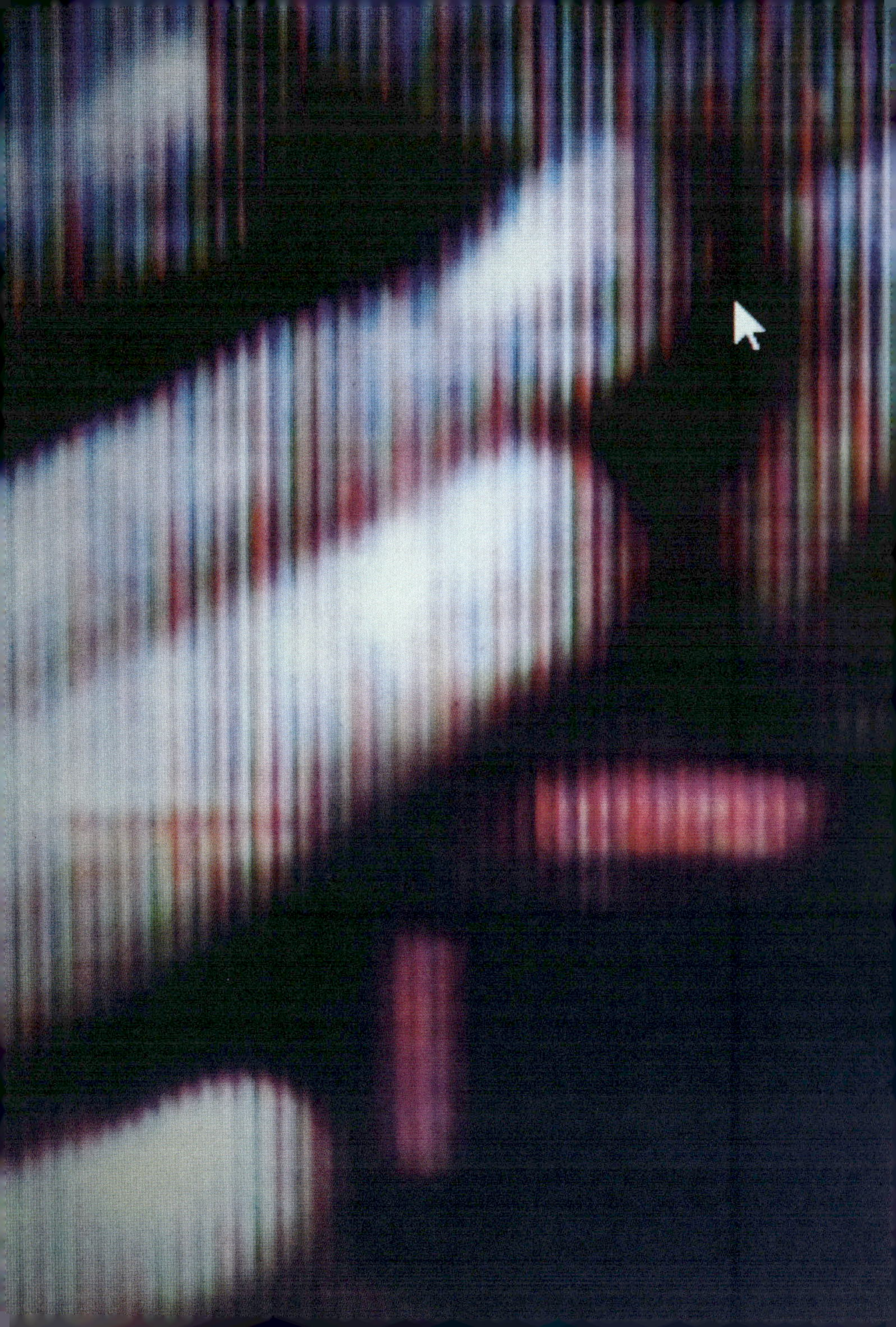

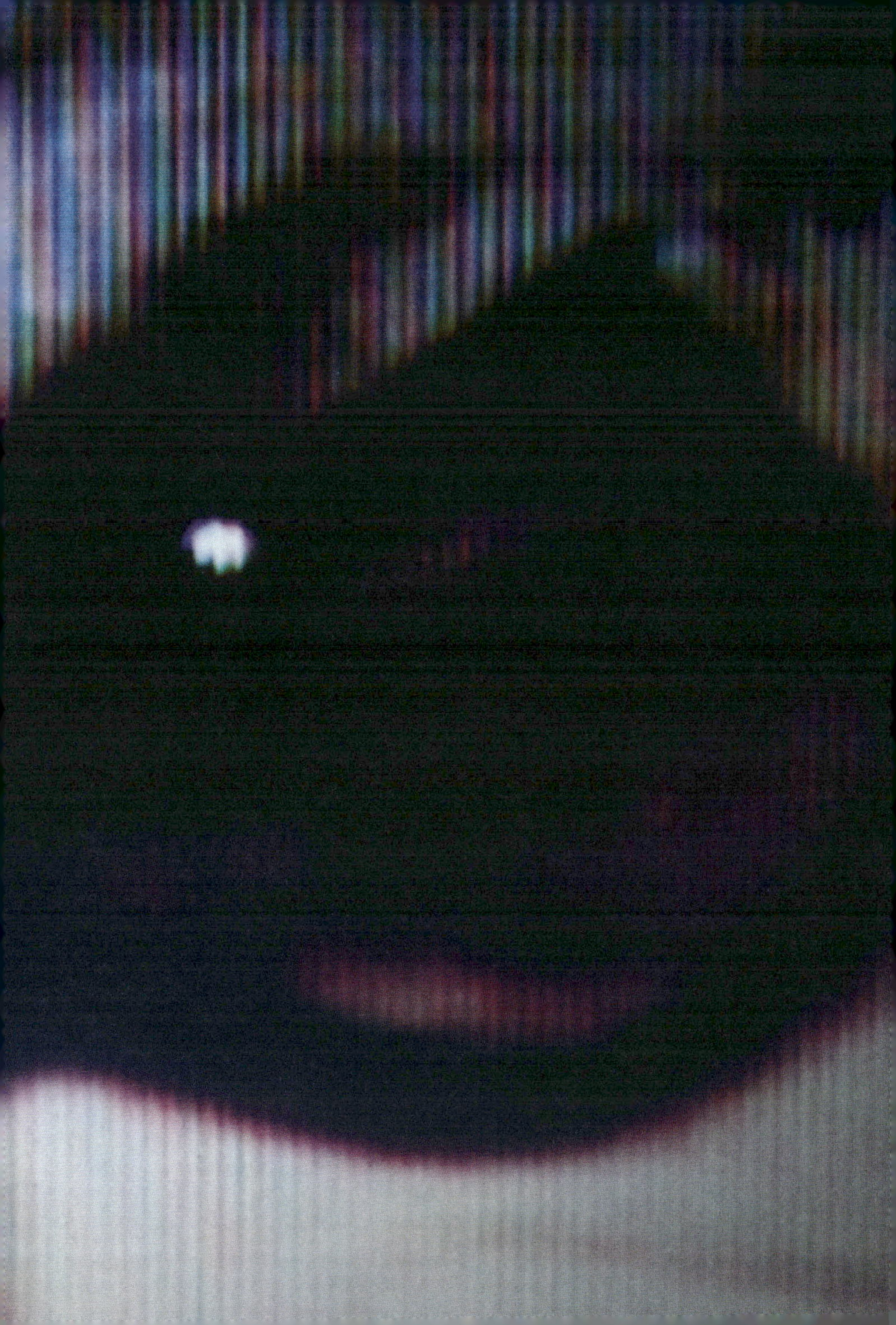

Scrolling
Scroll
Touch Sensitive
Close-Up
Hand
Hand Movement
Science Museum
London
Moiré
Interface
Participation
Interaction

Smart Phone
Portable Information Device
Photographing
Hand Holding Phone
Screen Capture
Text
Your Text Here
Dark Background
Window
Digital Shutter
Interface
Differential Focus
Close-Up

Film Still
Citizenfour
Edward Snowden
Sunglasses
Telephone
Using Telephone
Spying Scandal
Hong Kong
The Mira Hong Kong
Black Suit
NSA
Classified Information
Surveillance
Information

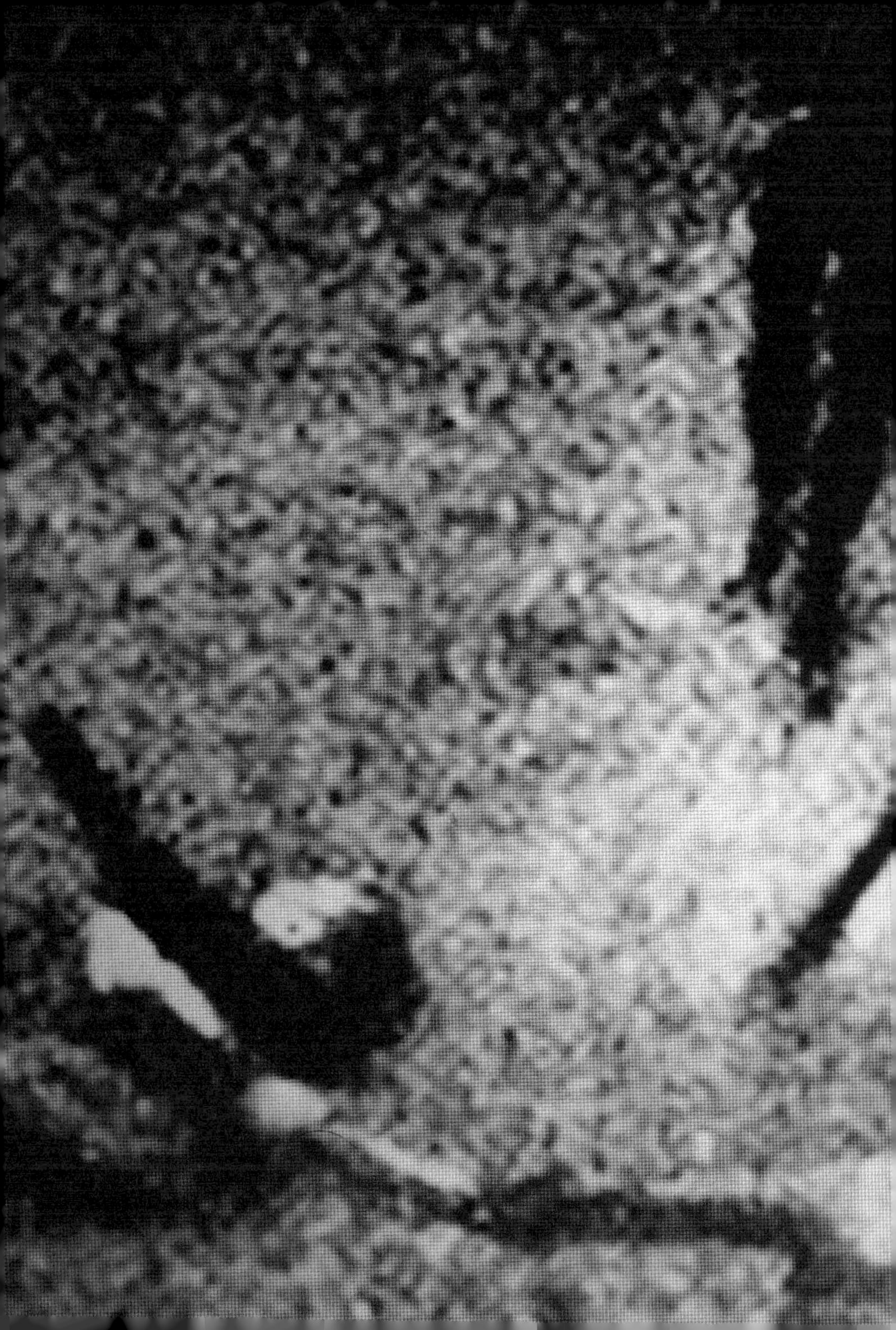

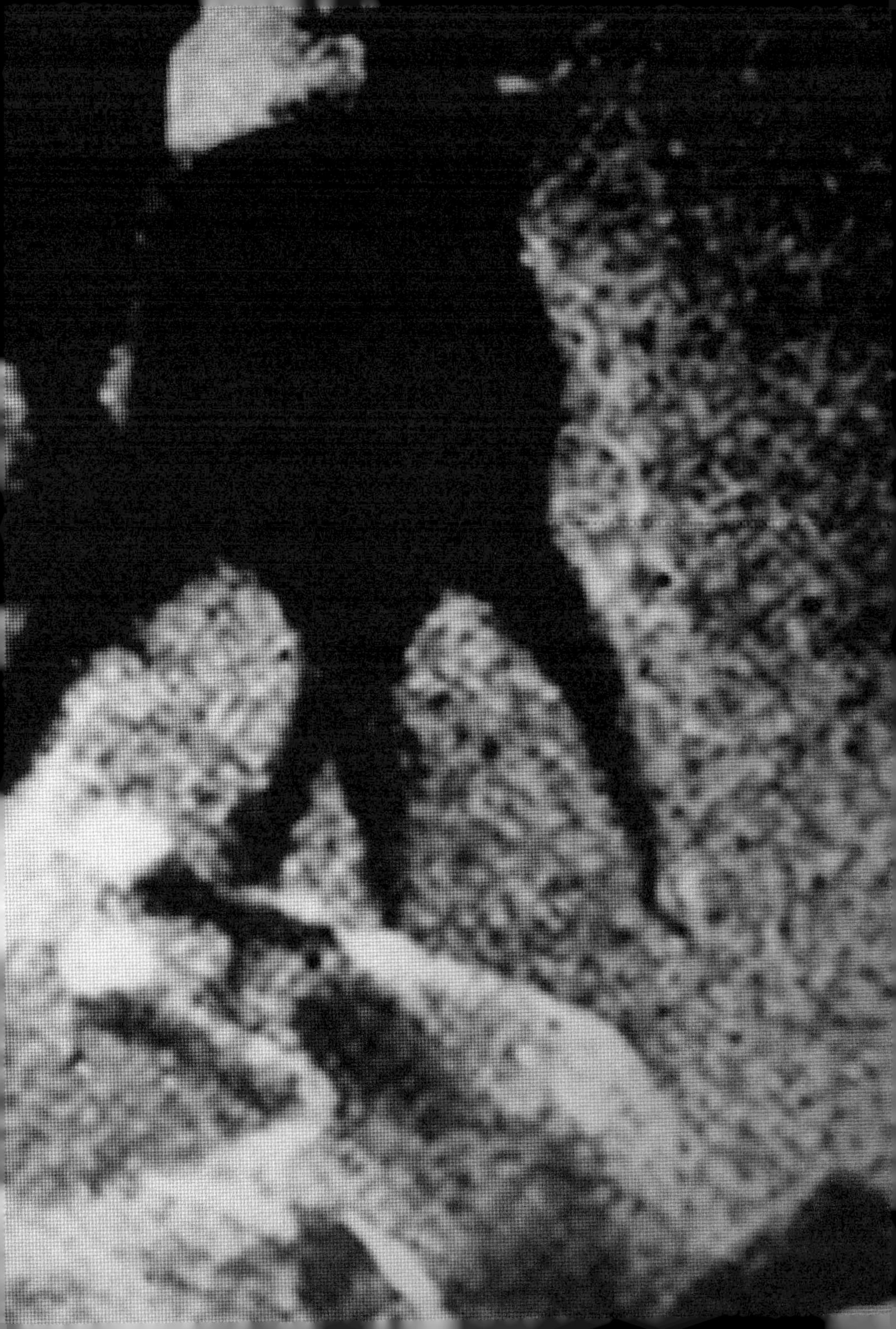

Hand Touching Keyboard
MacBook Pro
Mirroring
Image on Screen
Computer
Laptop
Matrix Data Waterfall
Keyboard
Stock Image
Left-Handed
Remote Control
Hacking
Data

Screen

wind-
off-
on-
pre-
multi-
-able
-er
-ed
pre-
-play
silk-
-writer
sun-
un-ed
smoke-

Smart Phone
Portable Information Device
Image on Screen
Tea
Kitchen Table
Wooden Surface
Chocolate Wrapper
Screen
Banana Skin
Multiple Portraits
Female
Head in Hands
Comparison

Film Still
Solarization
Gaze
Fortune Teller
Zoltar
Big
Wish-Making
Arcade Machine
Special Effect
Glowing Eyes
Red Eyes
Pepsi

Translation
Words on Screen
Tablet
Mini Tablet Computer
Nexus 7
Holding
Glass
Radiator
Portable Information Device
Night
Window
Artificial Light
Indoors

Giphantie
Google
Digitisation
Digitised Book
Tiphaigne de la Roche
1760
Novel
Fantasy Novel
Close-Up
Screen Capture
Moiré
First Part
French Literature
Proto-Photography

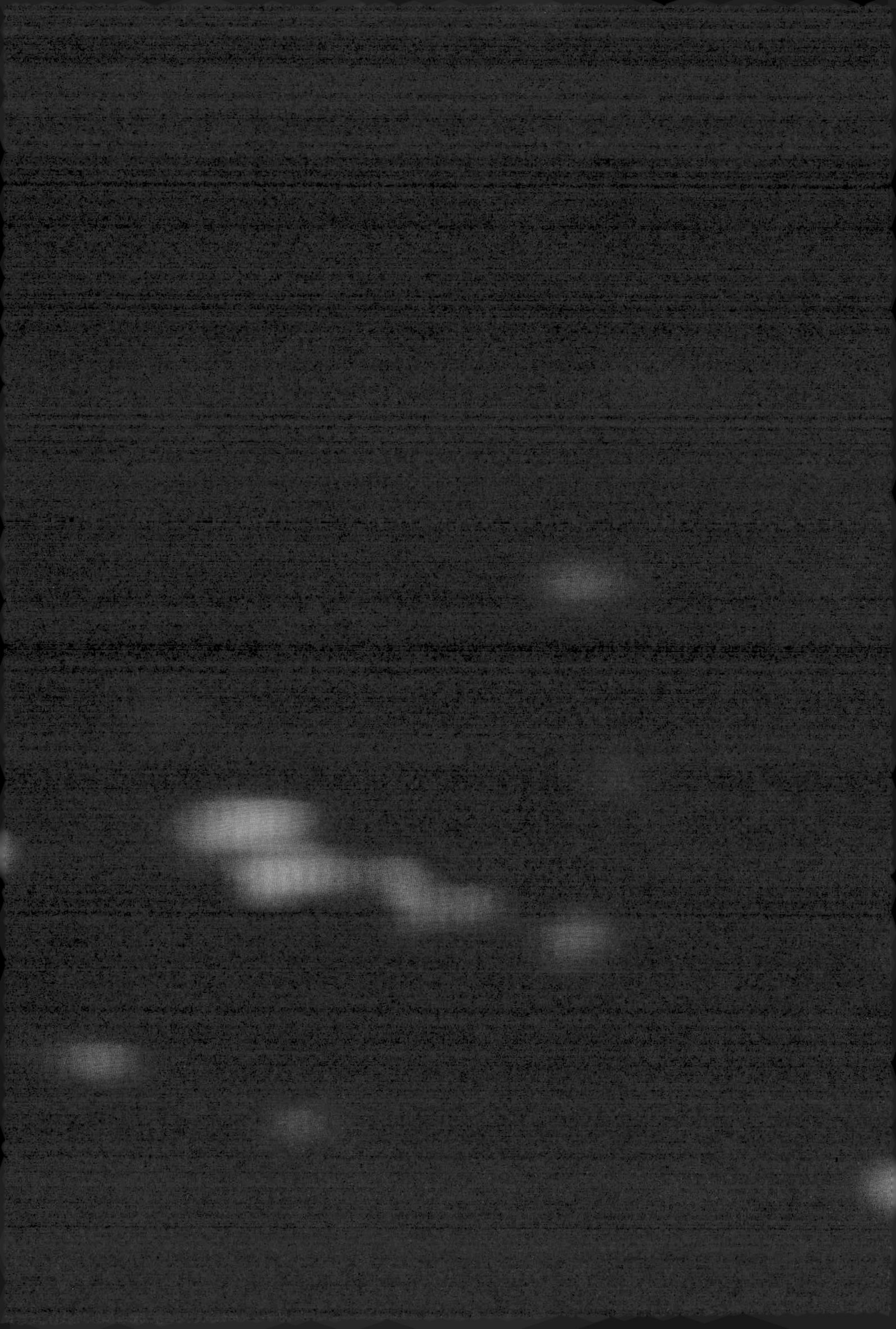

Photographing
Nokia
Lumia 920
Photographing Screen
Icons
Laptop in Background
Differential Focus
Holding
Hand
Close-Up
Microsoft Word
Word Processor
Text on Screen
Interface

Piano
Wooden Piano
Educational Video
Learning
Zimmermann
Tablet
Mini Tablet Computer
Nexus 7
YouTube
Black and White Keys
Portable Information Device
Made in Germany

Touch Sensitive

56.58	Staphylococcus aureus
29.07	Alternaria alternata
26.74	Aspergillus niger
20.93	Cladosporium sp.
10.47	Penicillium spp.
13.57	Staphylococcus epidermidis
8.01	Pseudomonas aeruginosa
7.73	Neisseria sicca
6.98	Aspergillus flavus
6.51	Micrococcus luteus
3.66	Proteus mirabilis
2.85	Bacillus subtilis
2.33	Aspergillus fumigatus
2.33	Rhizopus stolonifer
1.16	Aspergillus ochraceus
1.09	Enterobacter aerogenes

Smart Phone
Photographing
Photo Messaging
Close-Up
Portable Information Device
Human Hand
Extended Index Finger
<u>Touch Sensitive</u>
iPhone 4s
Ladies Entrance
Entrance Sign
Bilingual
Bricks
Tiles
Outdoors

Touching
Photographs
Family Album
Touching Screen
Flash Reflection
Touchscreen Gloves
Black and White
Portraits
People
History
Touch Sensitivity
Immersion
Ida
Film Still
Participation

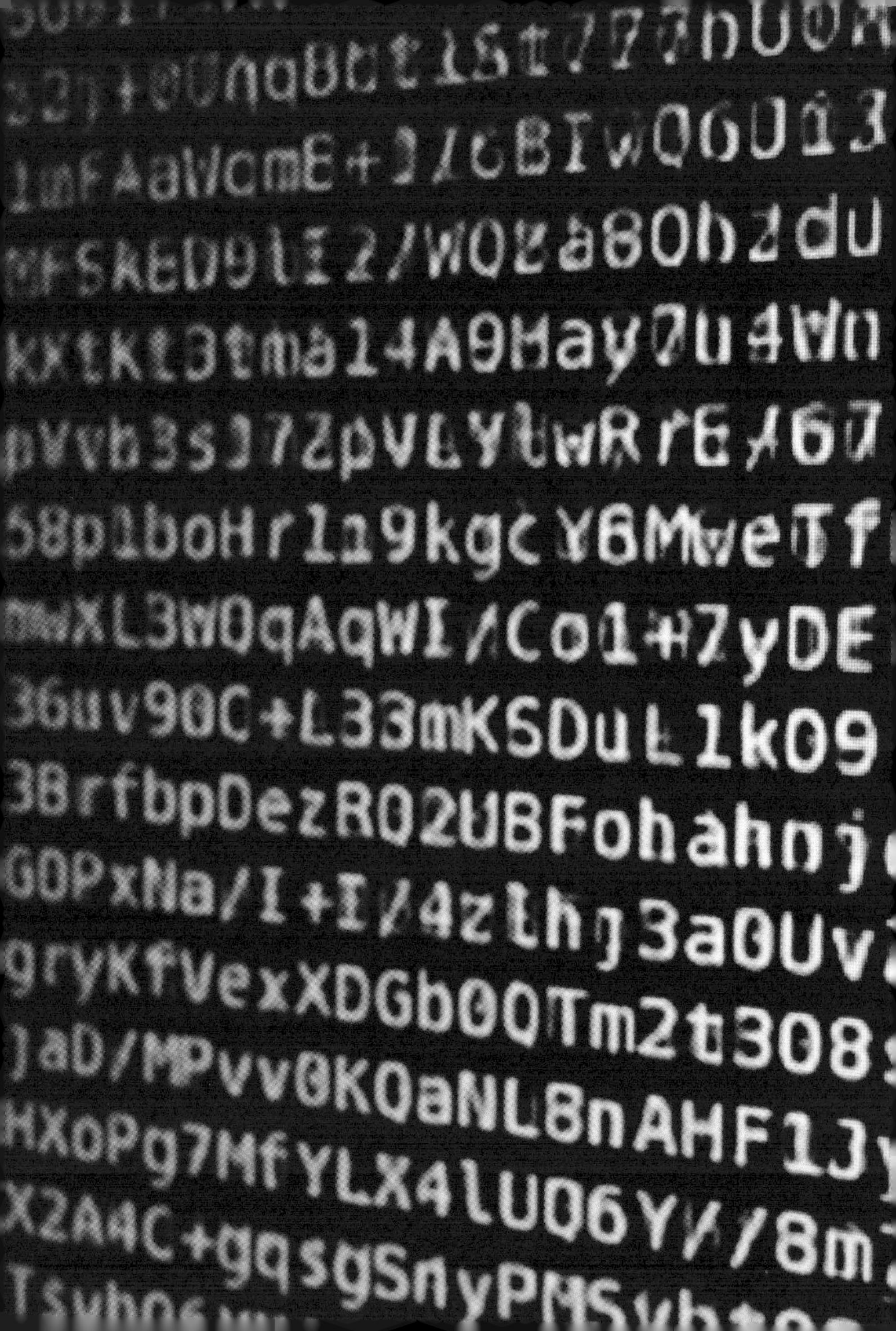

s2j+0UnqUEt1St77hU0A
1nFAaWomE+J/6BIwQ6U13
mFSkED9lI2/WOZa8Ob2dU
kxtkL3tma14A9Hay0u4Wn
pVvb3sJ72pVLYlwRrE/67
58p1boHrl19kgcY6MweTf
mwXL3W0qAqWI/Co1+7yDE
36uv90C+L33mKSDuL1k09
38rfbp0ezR02UBFohahnj
G0PxNa/I+I/4zthj3a0Uv
grykfvexXDGb00Tm2t308
JaD/MPvv0K0aNL8nAHF1J
HXoPg7MfYLX4lU06Y//8m
X2A4C+gqsgSnyPNSvbt
Tsyb06

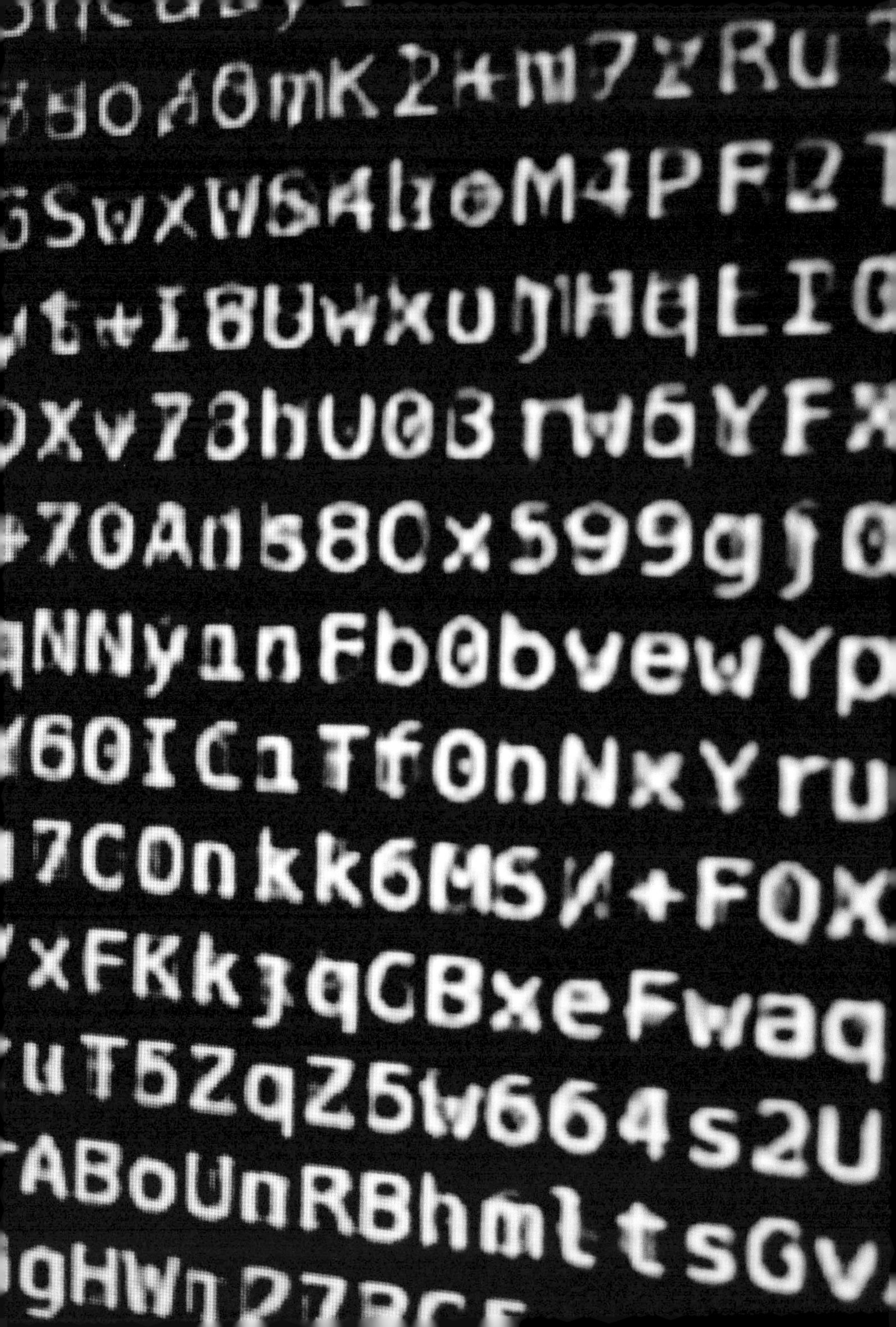

Gesture
Hand
Cultural Reference
Tablet
Mini Tablet Computer
Nexus 7
Touch
Virtual
Concept
Mirroring
Art History
Iconic

Smart Phone
Portable Information Device
Photographing
Photographing Art
Extended Index Finger
Hand Holding Phone
Statue
Park
Hedge
People in Background
Grass
Sky
Potsdam
Art History

Tablet
Mini Tablet Computer
Portable Information Device
Painting
Image on Screen
Peeling Apples
Apples
Woman
17th Century
Dutch Painting
Reynier Hals
Dark Background

Data

Baudrillard, Jean. Screened Out (Verso, 2014)
Flusser, Vilém. Towards a Philosophy of Photography (Reaktion Books, 2000)
Flusser, Vilém. Gestures (University of Minnesota, 2014)
Hand, Martin. Ubiquitous Photography (Polity Press, 2013)
Kember, Sarah; Zylinska, Joanna. Life After New Media (MIT Press, 2012)
Laruelle, Francois. The Concept of Non-Photography (Urbanomic, 2011)
Lister, Martin (ed). The Photographic Image in Digital Culture (Routledge, 2013)
McKenzie, Jai. Light and Photomedia (I.B.Tauris, 2014)
Pallasmaa, Juhani. The Eyes of the Skin (Wiley, 2008)
Rancière, Jacques. The Future of the Image (Verso, 2009)
Steyerl, Hito. The Wretched of the Screen (Sternberg, 2012)
Virno, Paolo. Déjà Vu and the End of History (Verso, 2015)

Nokia
Lumia 920
Smart Phone
Portable Information Device
Ok Button
Original
Saved
Reverting
Function
File
No Image
Interface
Data

Smoke Screen
Soldiers
Office
Differential Focus
Portable Information Device
Holding Phone
Smart Phone
Hand
Iraq
War on Terror
US Military
Red Smoke
Baqubah
Immersion

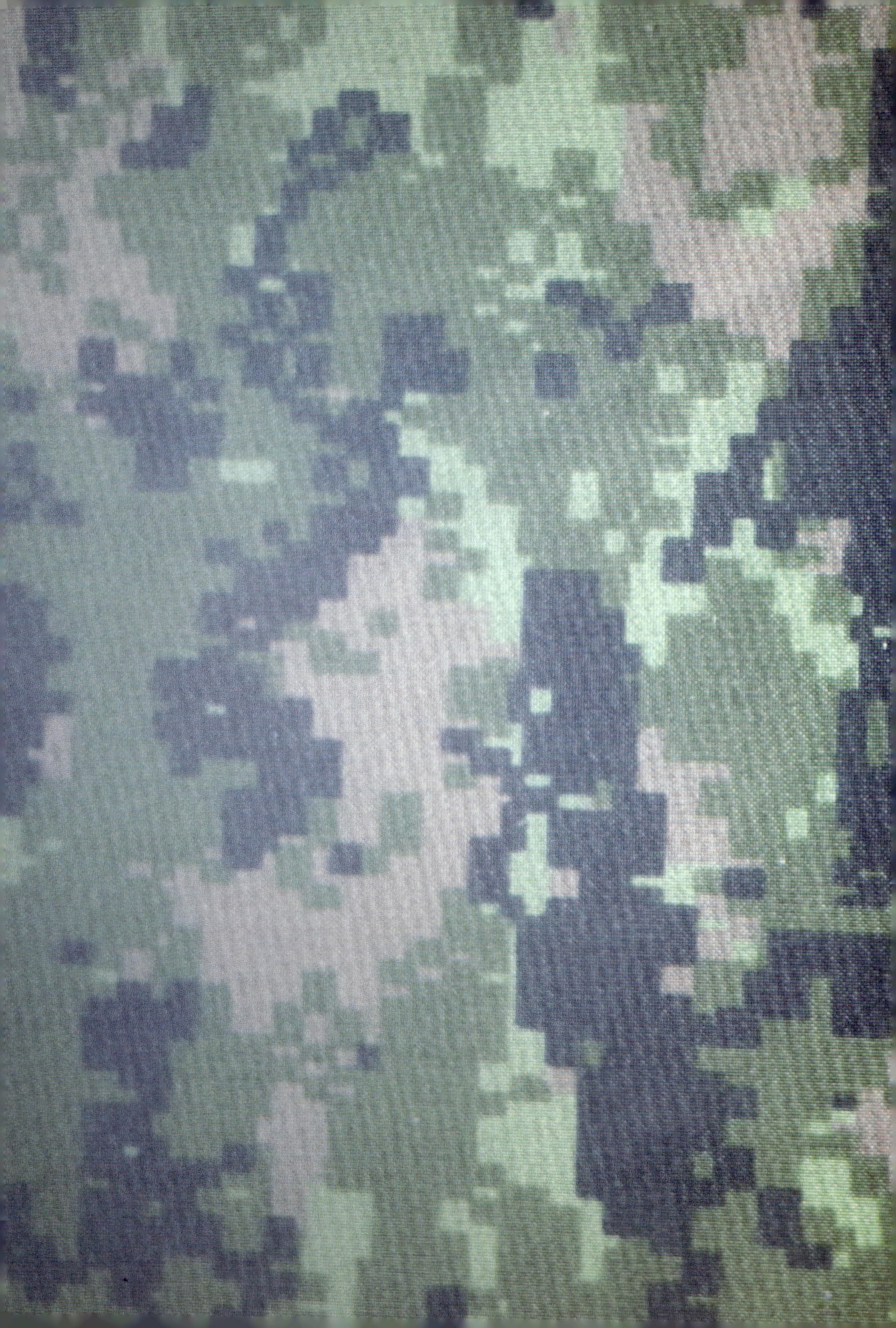

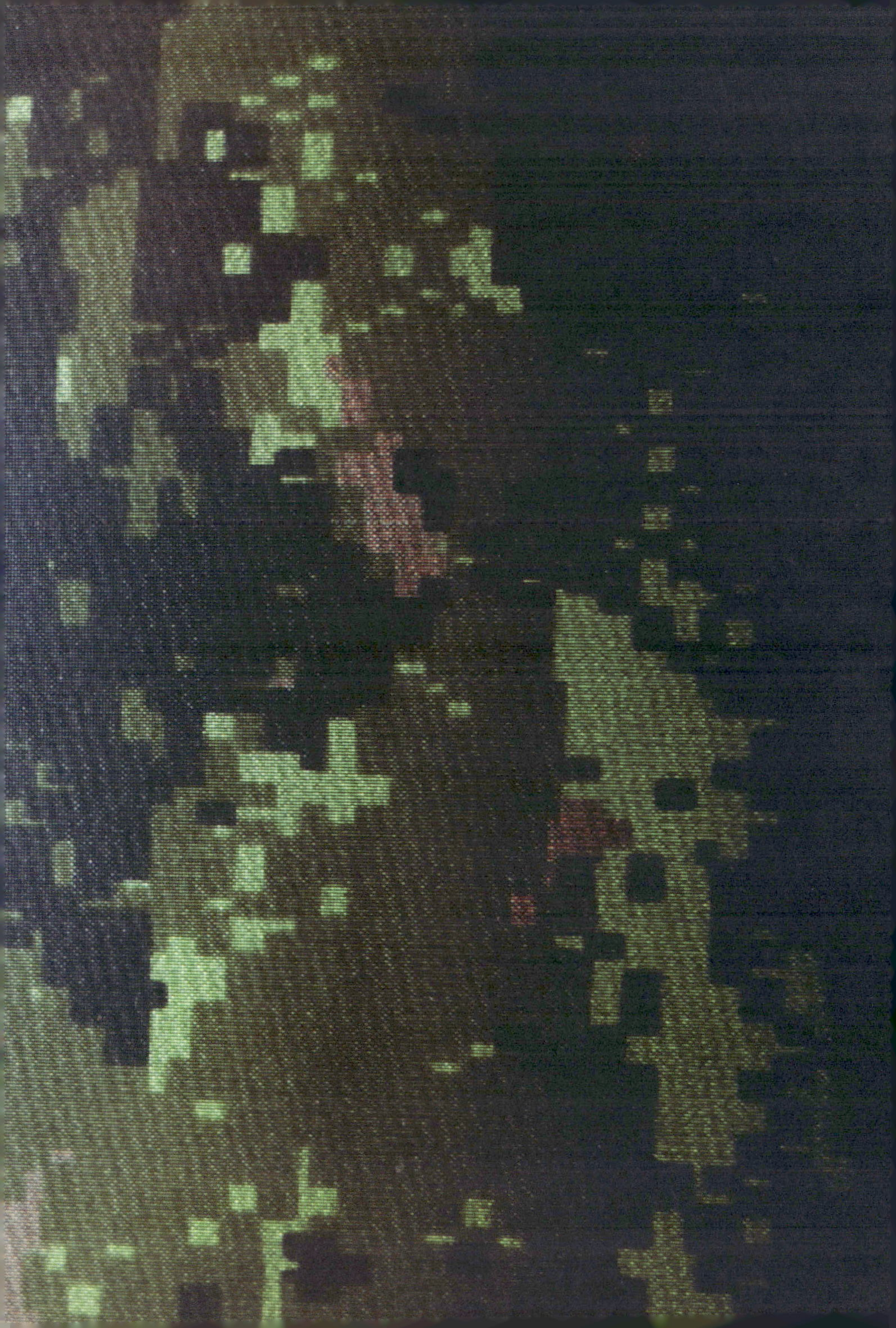

Index of Photographs

1

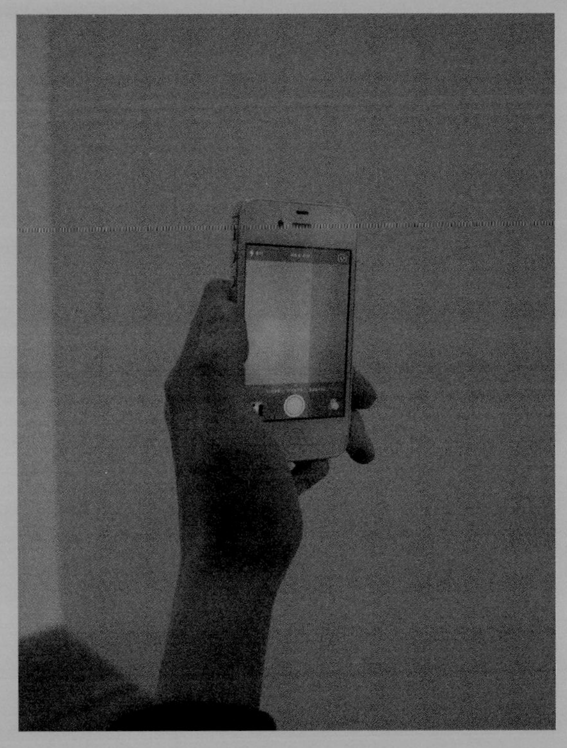

2

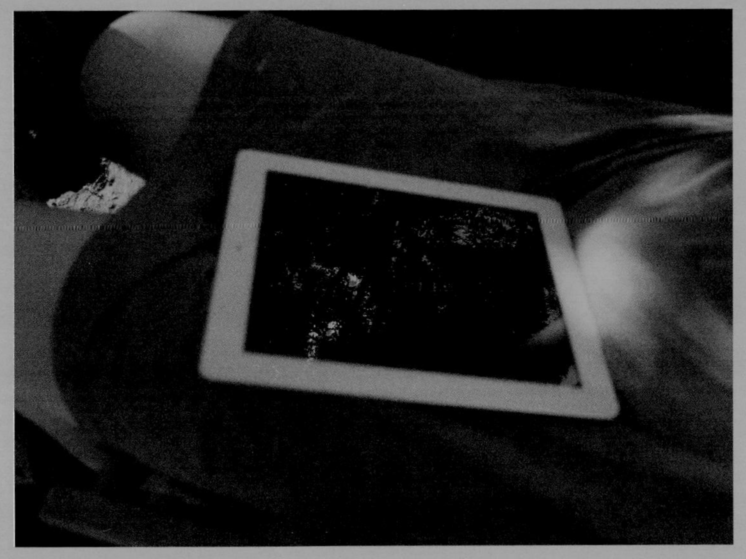

3

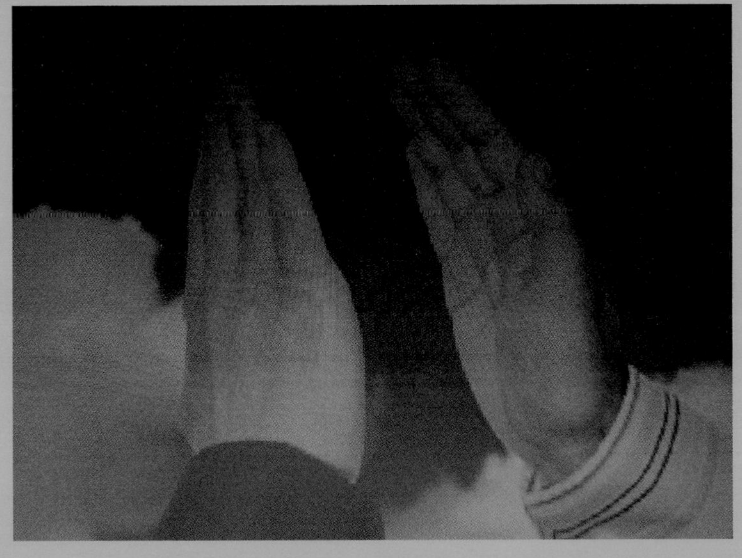

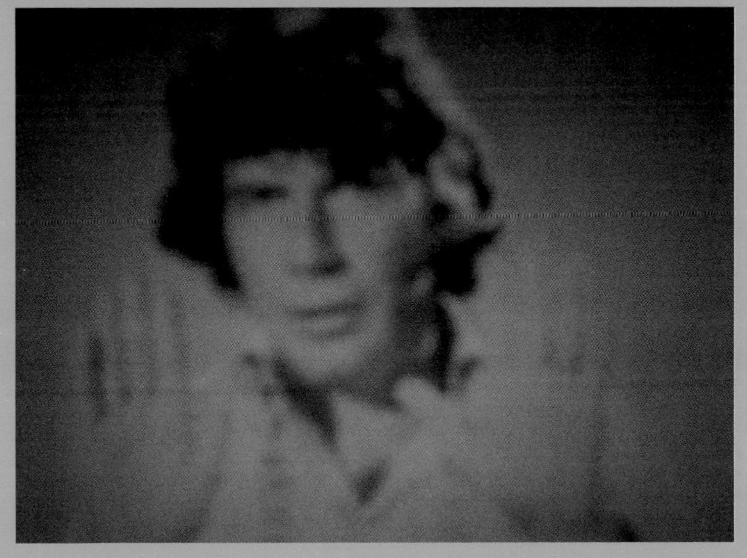

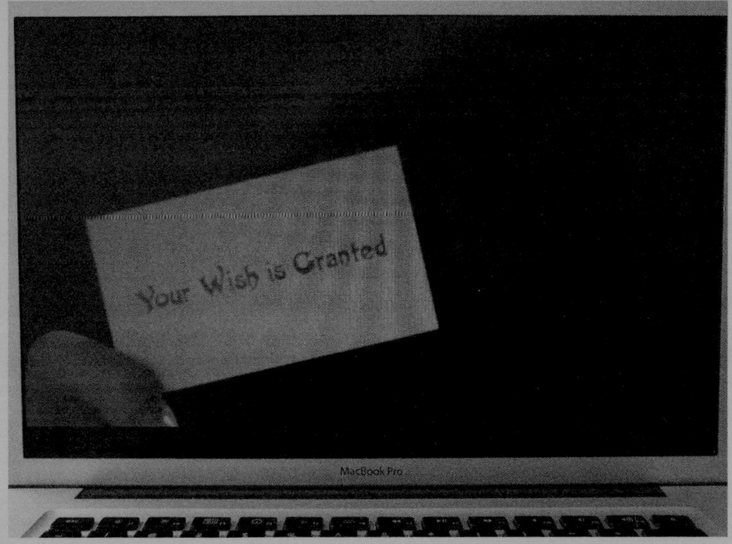
Your Wish is Granted
MacBook Pro

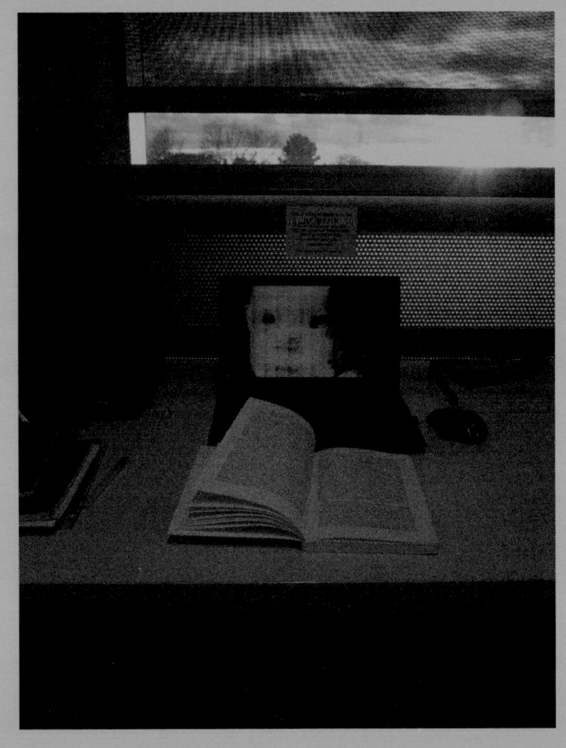

7

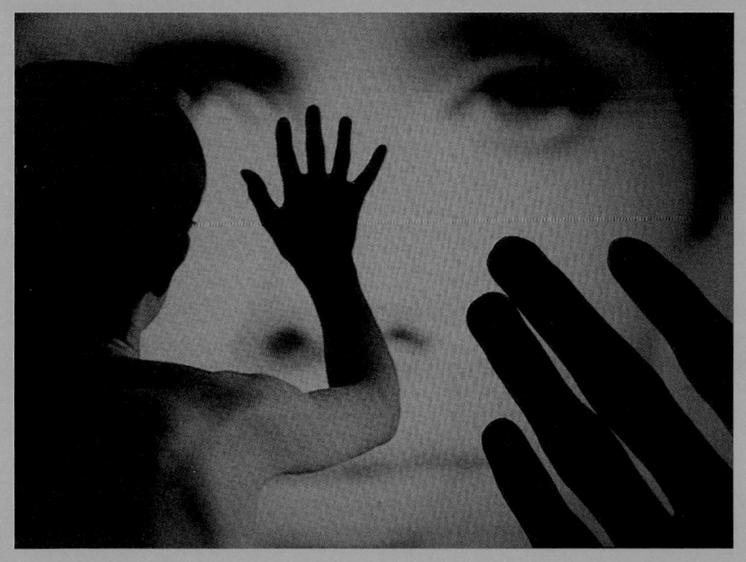

8

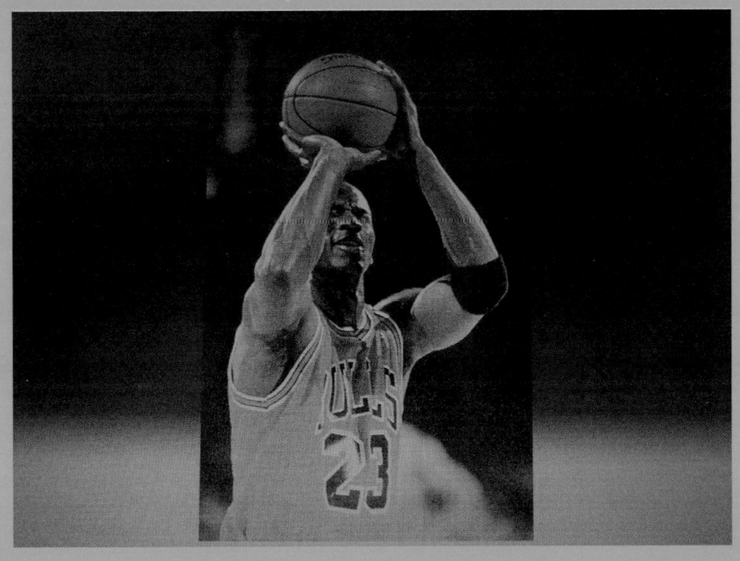

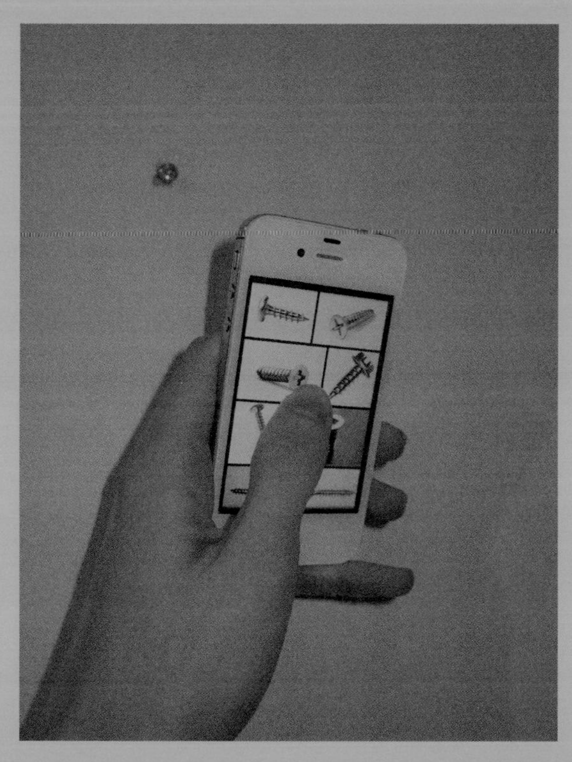

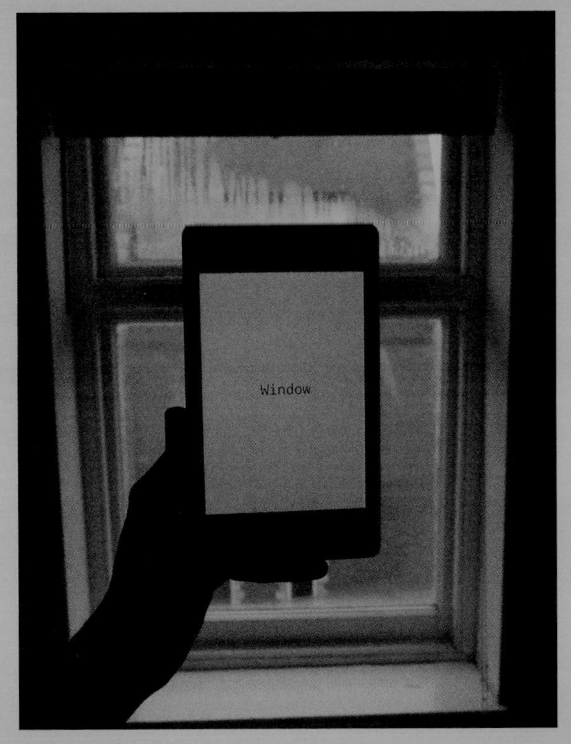
Window

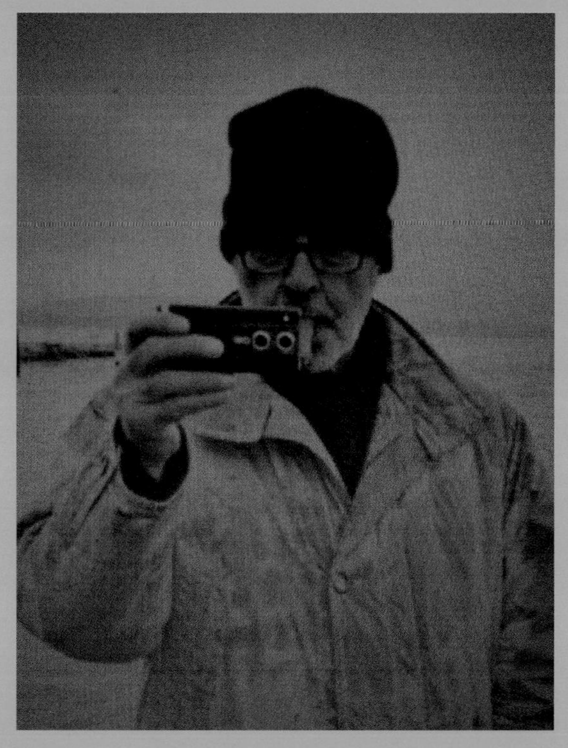

12

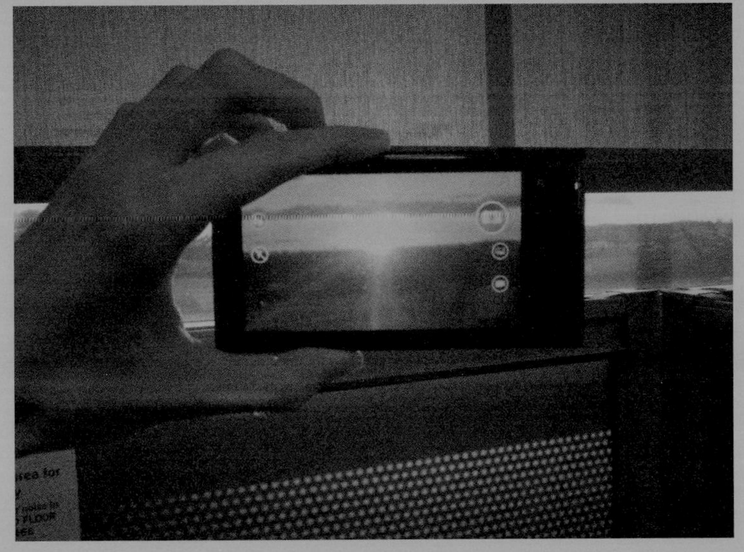

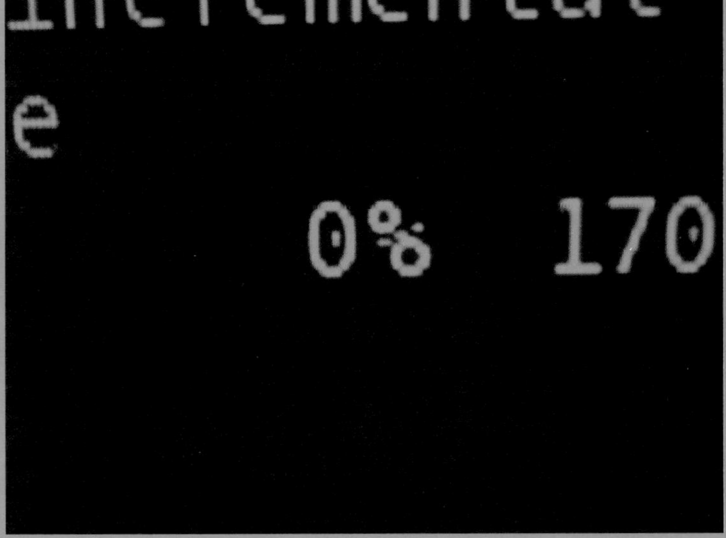
e
0% 170

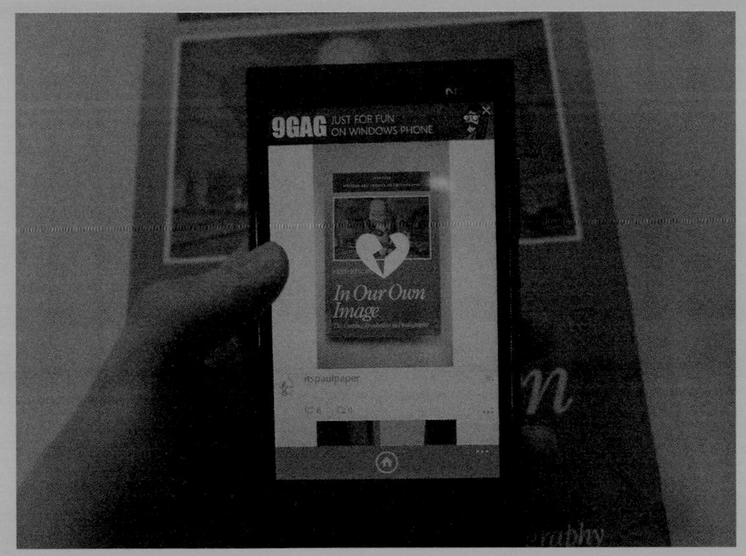
9GAG
JUST FOR FUN
ON WINDOWS PHONE
In Our Own
Image
itspaulpaper

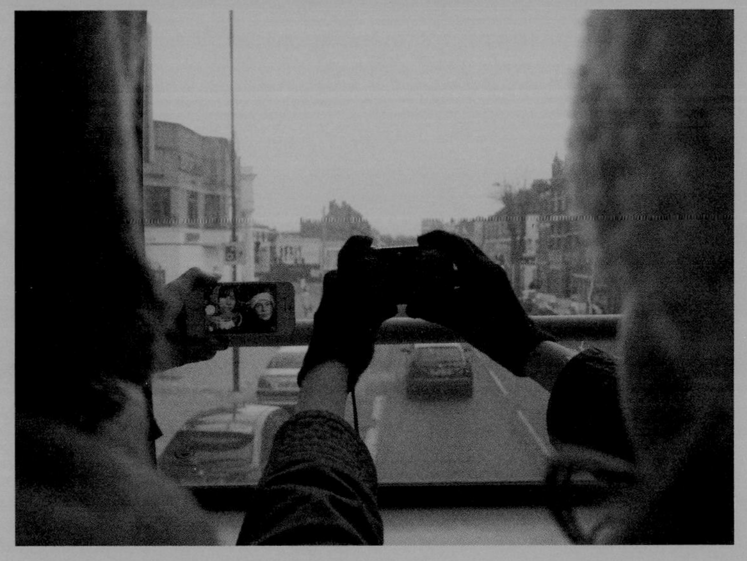

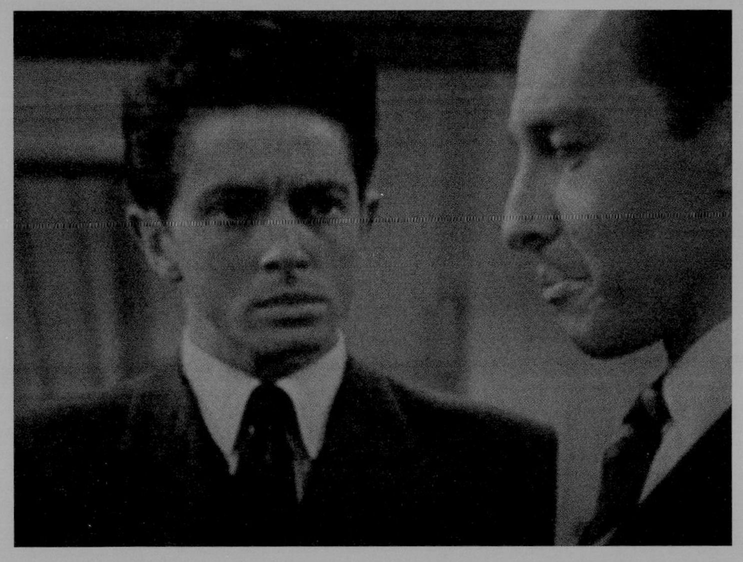

17

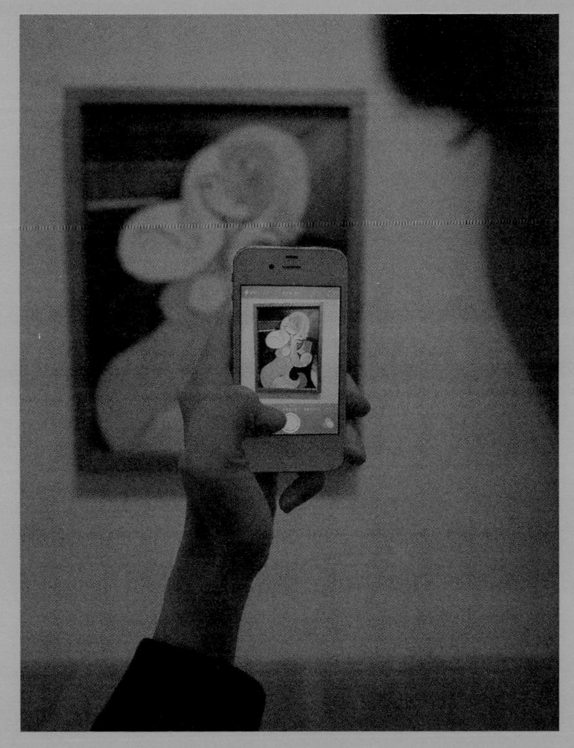

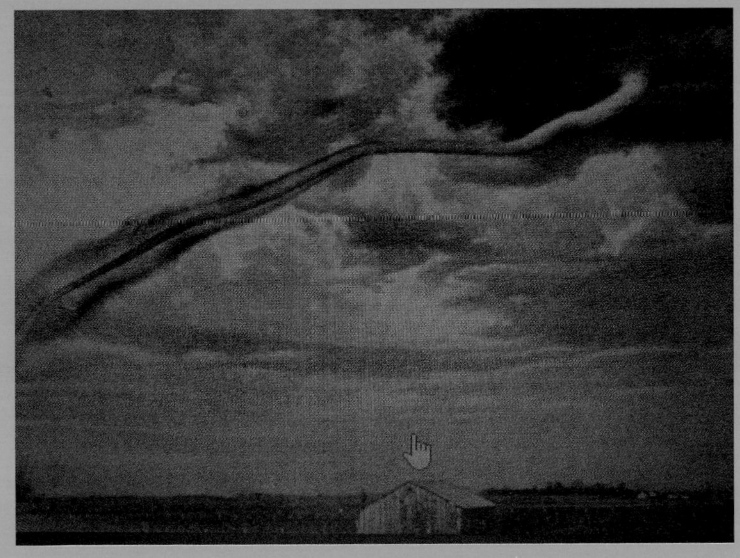

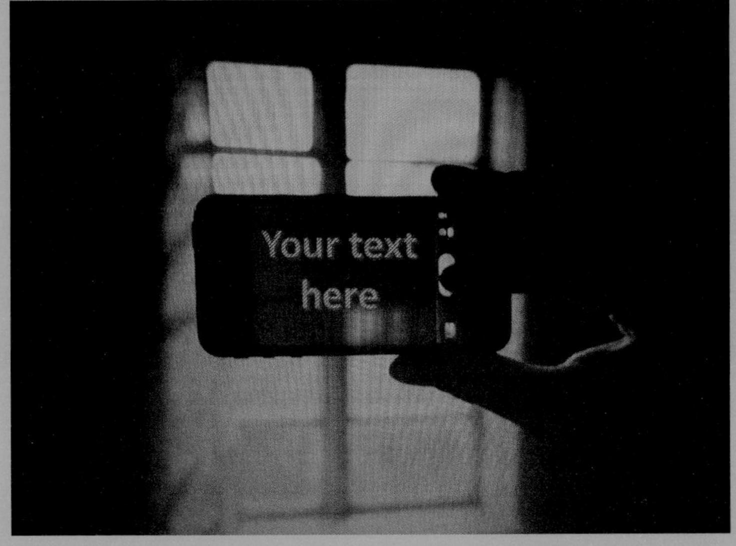
Your text
here

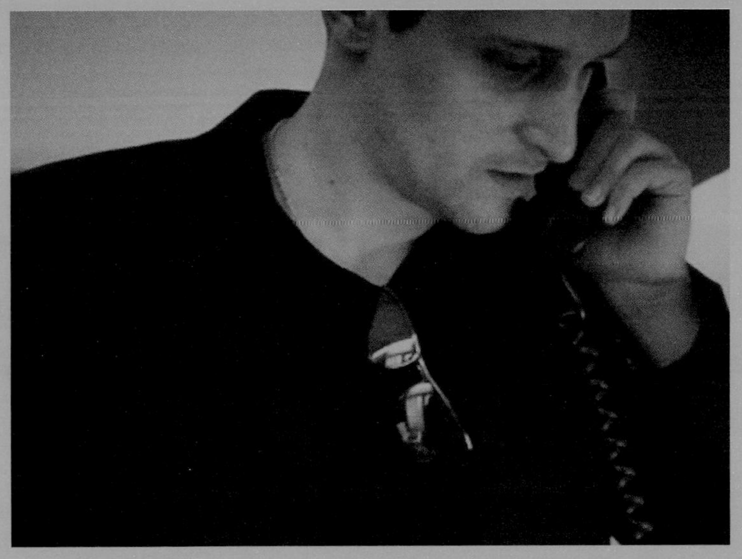

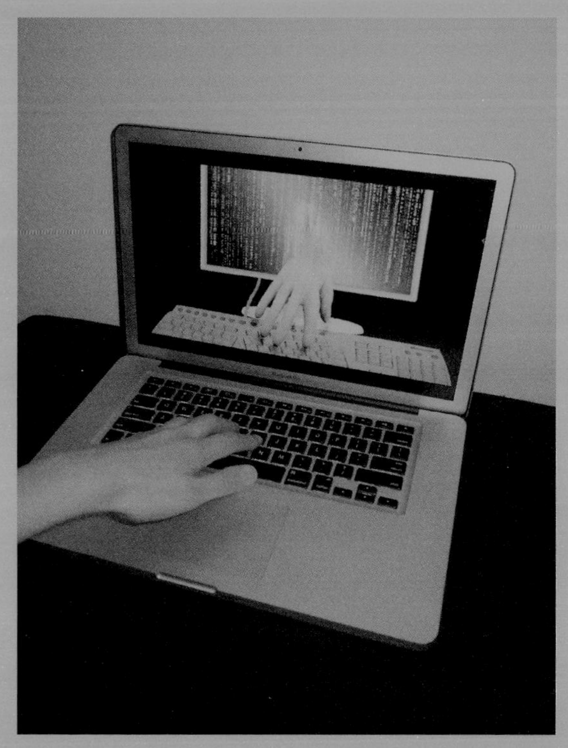

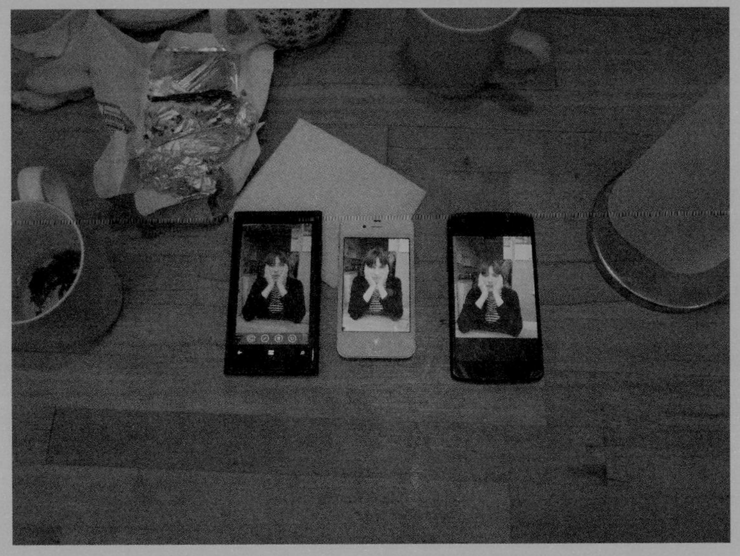

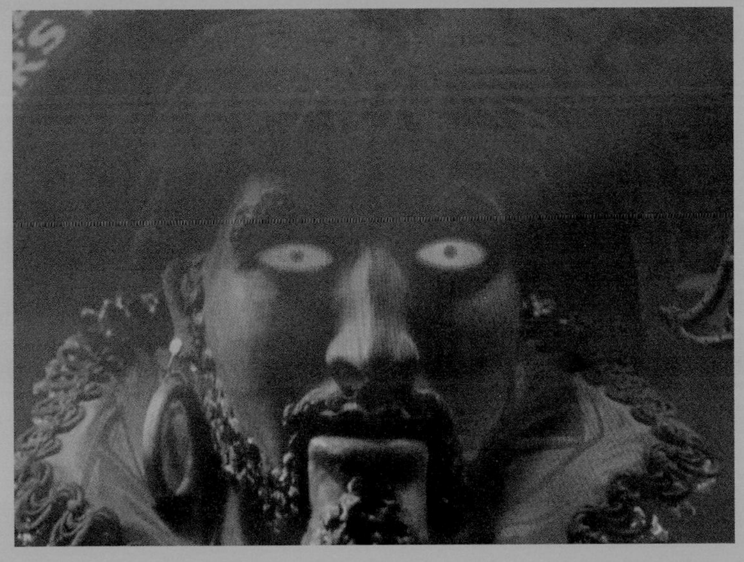

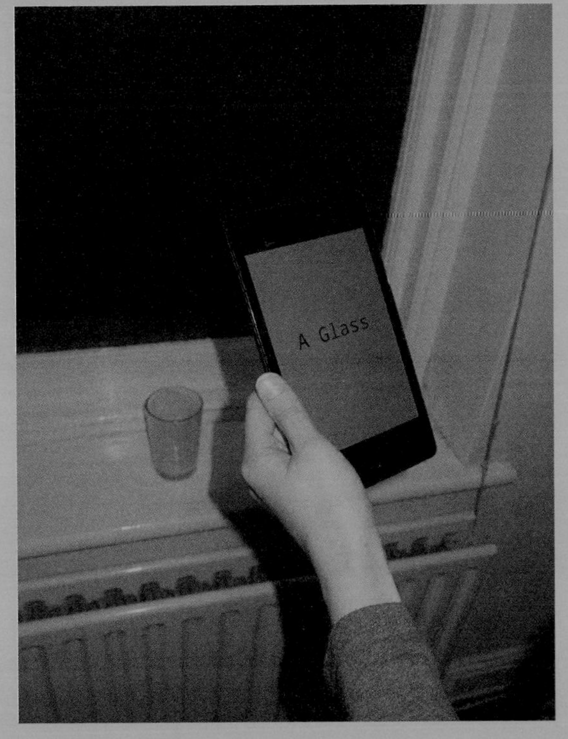
A Glass

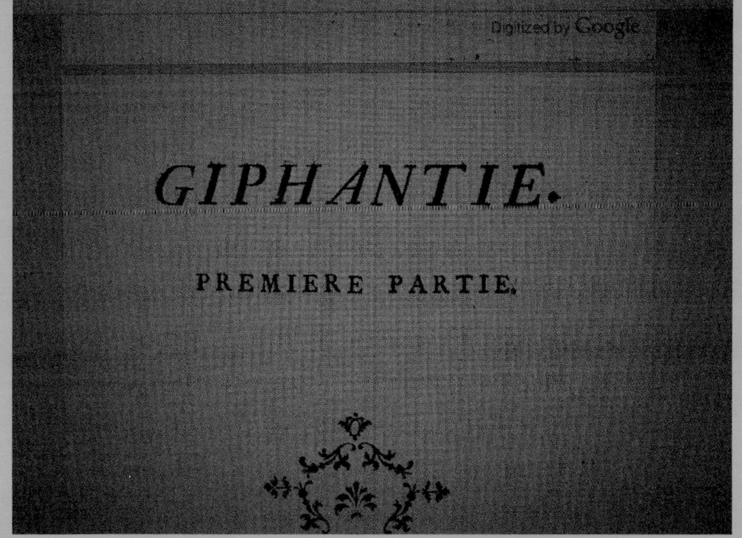

GIPHANTIE.

PREMIERE PARTIE.

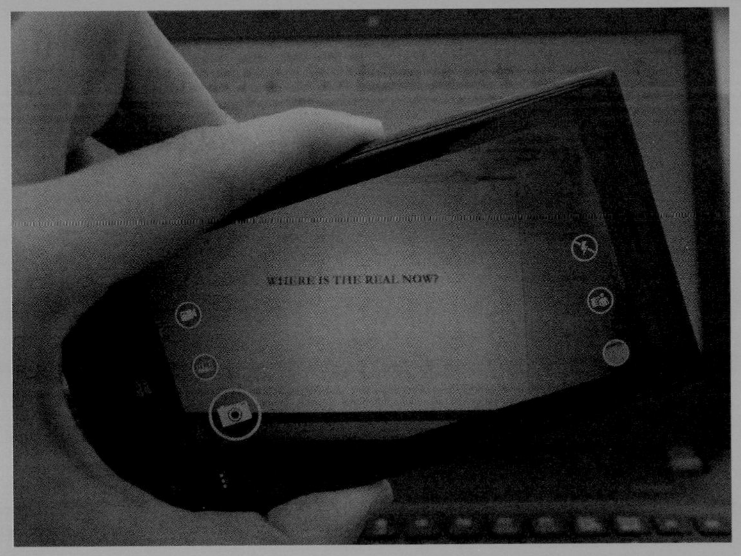
WHERE IS THE REAL NOW?

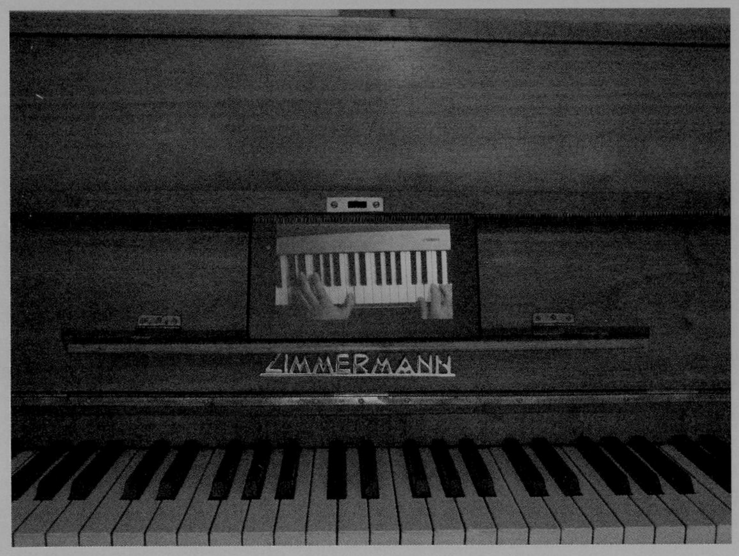
ZIMMERMANN

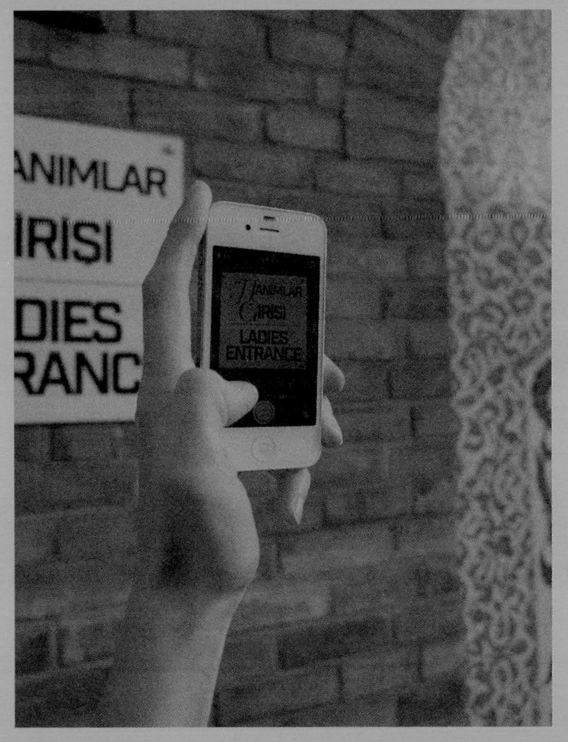
ANIMLAR
IRISI
DIES
RANC
LADIES
ENTRANCE

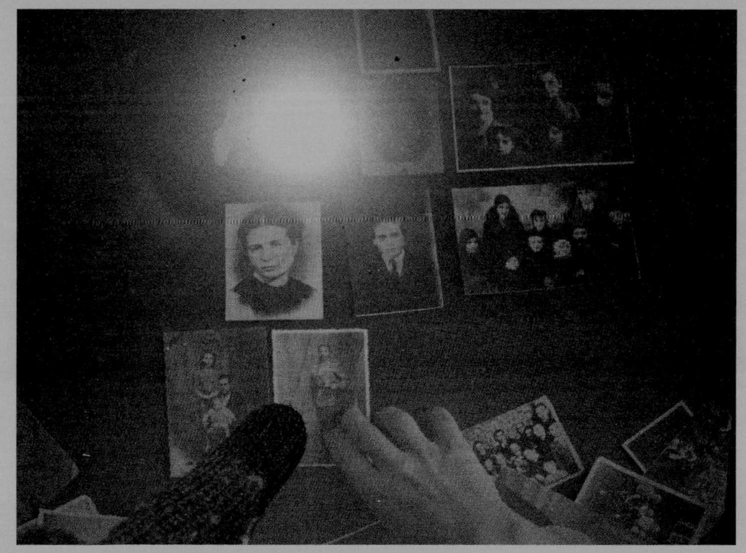

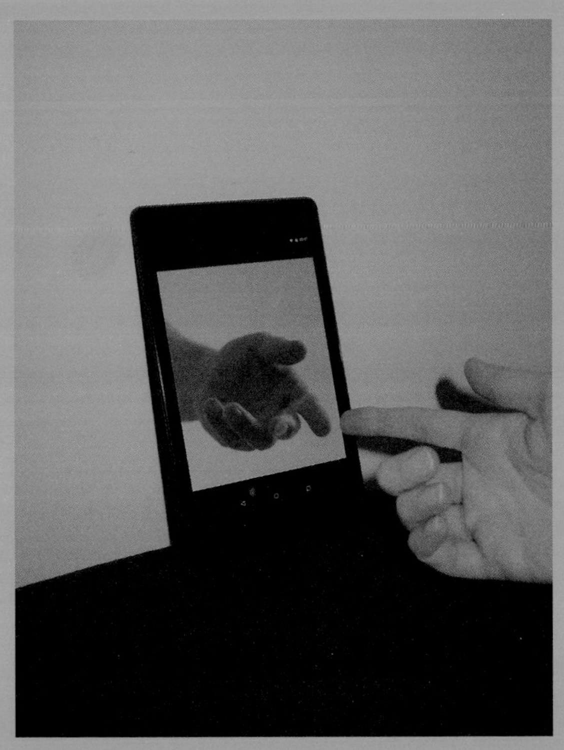

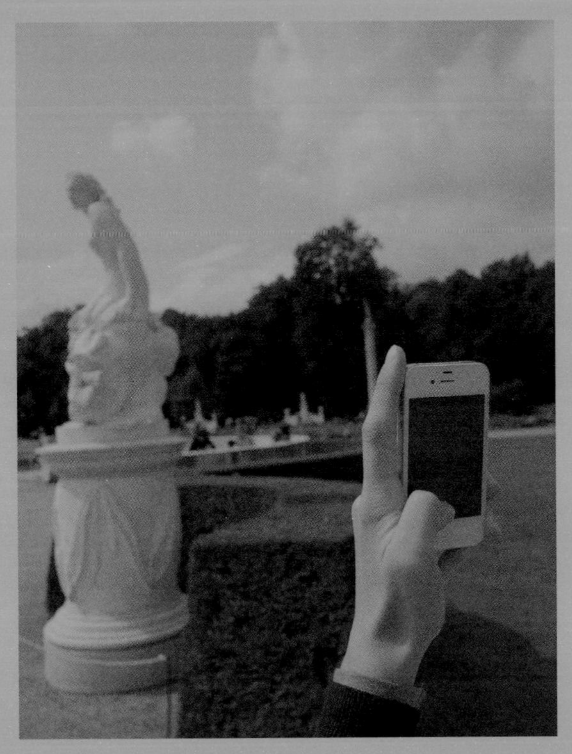

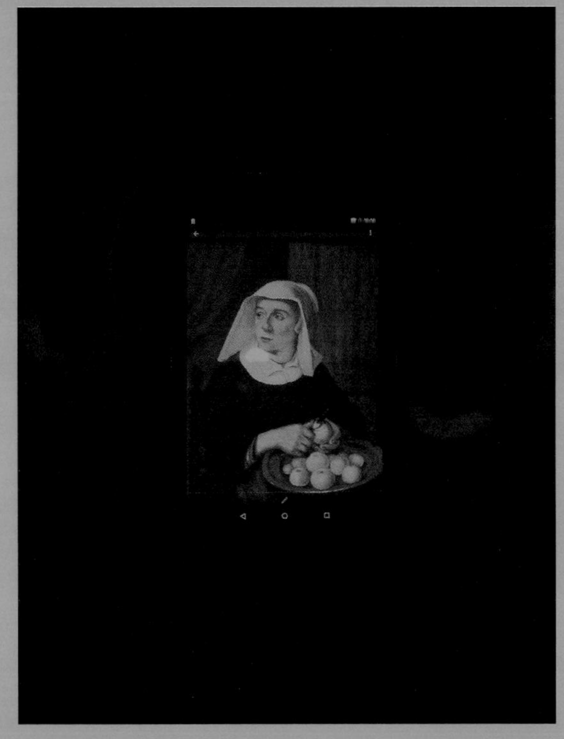

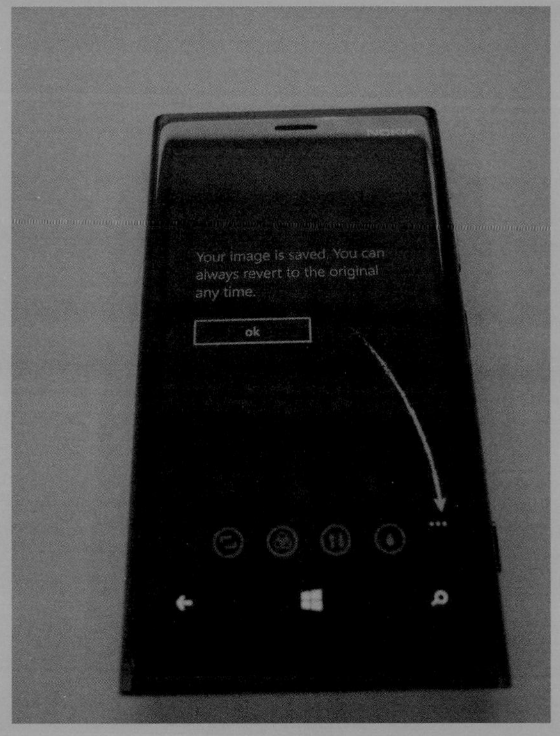
Your image is saved. You can
always revert to the original
any time.
ok

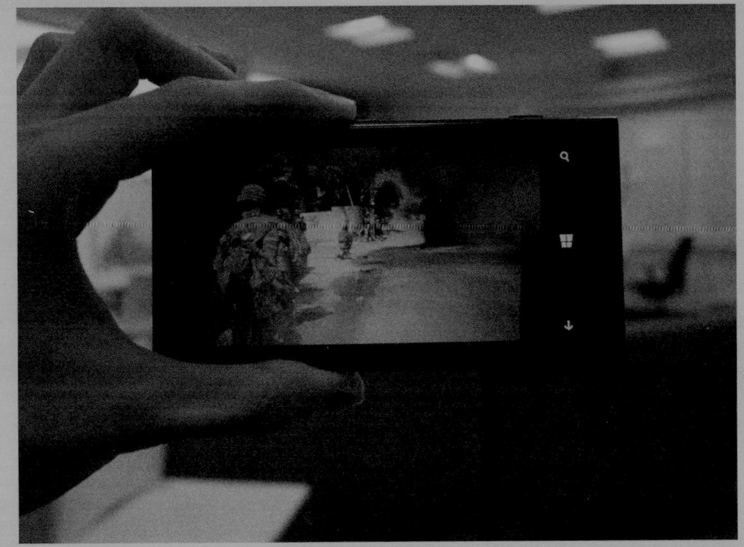

What does it mean to live in a world where the digital screen is so prominent? Smoke Screen is a subjective exploration into the conditions of a digital screenship. It is a curious look at the screen-empowered mediation and the abstract levelling of all information.

SMOKE SCREEN

Paul Paper

Edition of 200

Edit and design by Paul Paper and Lodret Vandret
Texts by Rowan Lear
Design concept by Fred Cave

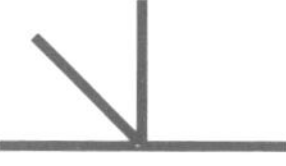

ISBN: 978-87-92988-13-3

Published in Copenhagen by Lodret Vandret, September 2015
Printed in the EU

www.lodretvandret.com